A Matter of Choice

A Matter of Choice

Pat A. Paulson

Sharon C. Brown

Jo Ann Wolf

Phoenix Rising Press

Glen Ellyn, Illinois

©1989 by Phoenix Rising Press. All rights reserved. No part of this book may be used or reproduced in any manner without written permission except in the case of brief quotations embodied in critical articles or reviews.

For information, address Phoenix Rising Press, P.O. Box 3088, Glen Ellyn, IL 60138.

This book is not intended for use in psychotherapeutic situations.

Library of Congress Catalog Card Number
88-92607

International Standard Book Number
0-944272-01-0

Printed in the United States of America

Edited and Designed by Kathleen D. McCleave

Original Cover Art, *The Open Door*
Oil by Maurice E. Paulson

Back Cover Photo by John D. Dove

To Our Parents

*Who instilled within us
a desire to make a difference*

**Hazel Annette Hamilton
George F. Hamilton**

**Bernice B. Brown
Wallace E. Brown**

**Helen M. Wolf
Joseph W. Wolf**

Beginning

Introduction	1
Learning	3
You	9
Choosing	15
Waking Up	21
Taking Charge	27
Selfishness	35
Change	41
Risk	47
Communication	53
Blame	59
Guilt	65
Worry	71
Fear	75
Approval	79
Trust	83
Perfect	87
Insight	93
Your Word	99
Practicing	105
Content	111
Caring	117
Sharing	121
Arguing	125
Forgiveness	129
Love	135
Problems	141
Falling In Love	147
Sex	151
Jealousy	157

Divorce	163
Children	169
Mothers	175
Fathers	181
Parents	187
Work	195
Money	201
Burnout	207

Mastering — 217
Your Story	223
Consideration	229
Expectations	235
Decisions	241
Habits	247
Thoughts	253
Commitment	259
Sexual Energy	265
Manifesting	271
Success	277
Miracles	283
Cooperation	287
Being Human	293
Good Will	299
Thankful	305
Getting Wiser	311

Concluding — 319
Index of Fundamental Misunderstandings	321
From Phoenix Rising	329

Introduction

Long ago we learned that life is a never-ending journey. Learning to recognize and honor our process raised many personal questions that demanded our attention. We combined our efforts and continued to search for answers that worked for all of us. We traveled many paths, always keeping in mind that life is very precious. Our desire is to be teachers of experience. Our goal is to teach the complexities of life simply and honestly. And our passion is to make a difference through our willingness to share what we have discovered.

Realizing that life is a process is a liberating experience. You move from learning to practicing to mastering—and mastering life is the greatest challenge. This book is divided into three sections related to that process. They contain chapters about yourself, chapters about your relationships, and chapters about being your best.

The process of **Learning** begins when you decide. You will find yourself wondering what you are about and how you need to do. This section teaches you to make choices that lighten your personal process of living. **Practicing** naturally follows as issues beg for your attention. Changes in your experience take place as you make honest choices and begin **Mastering** those problems that have forever seemed hopeless. They often disappear from your memory as you encounter new challenges on your journey.

A Matter of Choice is a book about your life process. It guides you into your inner world where you learn about your *self*. You will discover characteristics about yourself that want attention and need expression. Through acknowledgment, you give voice to your deepest desires, your deepest concerns, and your deepest wisdom.

Sometimes it is difficult to express words of appreciation because the gift received is so powerful. With this in mind, we want to acknowledge and extend our gratitude to Kathleen D. McCleave, our editor. Unconditionally, she has contributed, been our advisor, and inspired us with her enthusiasm. And to Maurice E. Paulson, our cover artist, who has never, for one moment, lost faith in us. He has been our mediator, our example, and our friend.

Learning

A fundamental misunderstanding
about learning
is that life
has correct answers somewhere.

Learning

Do you ever wonder who makes up the rules that are supposed to fit for all people? Do you believe that the circumstances of your life leave you with few choices? Has experience proven to you that life does unto you without your active participation? Surely, it seems odd that some events arrive in your life when you have done nothing to deserve their unpleasant consequences. Pondering your present situation, do you conclude that you are a victim of circumstances—you fervently wish you had made different choices; you hope that your circumstances somehow will change?

—Perhaps you feel hopelessly stuck in an unpleasant relationship.

—Perhaps you feel trapped in a job you hate but you have no choice because it pays good and you have so many responsibilities.

—Perhaps you have physical issues that so consume your life, you believe you have no choice about living.

—Perhaps you have lived asleep for so long that everything that could trap you has.

Sometimes it seems as if the only thing you can do is to wish and hope—wish life would be kinder and hope tomorrow will be easier. You hope your partner will get better or wish your partner would understand you. Or maybe you wish your present person would go away, and you hope the new one will arrive soon thereafter. You hope for a better job opportunity, and you wish you had credentials that would enable you to apply. You wish you could be successful, and you hope that someday it all will be different.

Perhaps you don't realize that life will continue to drive you until you wake up and take charge. Most of the input you have had in your life is about how things will be just fine if only you are good enough or if only you do what you should do. But have you ever noticed that when others are telling you how to live and be, their ideas are always based on conclusions about some generic *best* way to live life.

—You are told you should have a "good" job so you apply for the job that pays the most money. You plan your entire career around social status when you would rather be a forest ranger.

—You are told you should marry the "right" person. But the one you love has the wrong religious beliefs, the wrong credentials, the wrong ambitions, and besides they were born into the wrong life.

—You are told you should eat "healthy" food, so you buy only stone-ground, seven-grain bread even though the kernels stick in your teeth and it falls apart when you try to make a sandwich.

—And, of course, you have to live in the "right" neighborhood even though your mortgage payments will leave you financially pressed for the rest of your life.

You are, in fact, told how to live every facet of your life and what you should do in every life situation. So you do it that way, and then you spend the rest of your life wishing and hoping things would be just as fine for you as promised.

Well, wishing and hoping are activities of the mind that keep it occupied when you choose to ignore what really is happening to your life. Wishing and hoping are delusions that limit your choices. No matter how easy it seems, letting others determine the choices you make is the most difficult way to live. You end up living the choices that enhance their life. So what you have then is that *they* are having a great life.

Consider you and your life when you make your choices if you want to have a life that *you* care about living. When you really get that life is about what to do about you, your choices become clearer. You get to know yourself and what you want to do intimately.

You keep *you* in the forefront of your mind always wondering what is the best choice for this person you are going to spend all of the rest of your life with.

When you are looking for and choosing what adds to your life, you become your own advisor. You are the one that has your best interest in mind. You are the one that you will have to live all of the moments of your life with. You can quit relationships, jobs, children, and relatives but you cannot quit yourself. You are the only one who will wake up every day in your life.

You want more than wishing and hoping your life will get better. You want it better now. And the only way for it to get instantly better is for you to get in charge by making your own choices. The point is to get to choice and to choose as soon as possible. When you get to choice, you are in charge of what happens in your life. Knowing you have choices and making them gives you all the control you need to have your life go in the direction that you need and want it to go.

*A
fundamental
misunderstanding
about*

You

*is that you are
what you know,
what you have,
or what you do.*

The moment you were born you began to collect an identity. Some would say your identity is written in your name, others would say your identity is written in the stars. Perhaps you have taken personal profile tests, been psychoanalyzed, had your palm read or faithfully followed a mentor's instructions in an attempt to discover your identity.

Once the quest has begun, you will find yourself wanting to know more about you and about your life. Who you are, beyond the ways you have always identified yourself, becomes an immediate question. Your search for self-knowledge will lead you to pose questions that are difficult to ask and even more difficult to answer.

—You may question your experience of living.

—You may question how you came to have your particular beliefs and values.

—You may question what your responsibilities are.

—You may question the present direction of your life.

—You may question what you want and why you want it.

—You may question why you aren't getting what you want.

—You may question why you are with others the way you are.

—You may question why you love some and not others.

—And you may question yourself and your answers.

All that you thought was important holds little significance to you in this new arena. There will be times that you feel hopelessly puzzled and frustrated. When you ask questions about your identity, you will be tempted to want others to give you answers. You will be tempted to choose answers that agree with their definitions. You may be desperate for any answers as you notice your definition of yourself changing.

Your questions about your life path may take you into unfamiliar territory. You may resent having to be there. You may feel like a tourist and still find yourself intrigued with the new landscape. When you finally return to your familiar path, you may discover it no longer holds your interest so you willingly follow along the new path. However you find yourself questioning, you will discover answers—some that you love, others that you find difficult, and some so unbelievable you will wonder if you are in the same life.

Interestingly, whether you actively question your identity or whether you are thrust into questioning, the process of life will naturally urge self-discovery. On all levels, your physical, emotional, mental, and spiritual self will be challenged to question and discover because the issue of self-discovery is a natural process. Life always presents you with situations that leave you no choice but to question. Fortunately, you will find that you do have answers, and those answers will be ones that provide guideposts for you on this new, yet strangely familiar path. You will discover a you that you respect and appreciate, a you that you can count on, and a you that you can love.

Choices

Your questions bring you to self-discovery about your identity. The choices you make always influence your experience of your *self*. Some choices you make bring you the experience of your *self* as heavy or dark. Other choices you make bring you the experience of light.

How do you recognize and experience your *self* as light? How do you claim your birthright to be light?

Every time you choose light, you are light. You recognize that you are light and others recognize that you are light. This is a you that is radiant not heavy, a you that chooses to be unburdened not laden. This lighter you directs. It gives you the feeling of airiness and freedom. This lighter you penetrates darkness and restores sight and has enough energy to warm the coldest heart—to refresh and restore at the end of your storms. When you choose light,

—you are light in every sense of the word;

—you are light as a beacon signaling direction;

—you are light as one unburdened, without effort and struggle;

—you are light as the calm after the storm;

—you are light as a newborn without grief or sorrow;

—you are light as a teacher who enlightens;

—you are light as an artist who brings gladness and cheer;

—you are light as a messenger of good will;

—you are light as unconditional love.

When you are light, your job has miraculous success. When you are light, your relationships are smooth and loving. When you are light, your health improves and you feel great. When you are light, you are blessed with the emotions of joy and gladness. When you are light, your troubles are challenges. When you are light, you like you.

Nature's gift to you is the gift of choice. Each thought, each action, each encounter gives you the option to choose light. It will be a great challenge to choose light. Every time you do, you will be on your life path. You will be all of the things that lightness promises to bring.

> *The nature of unawareness is self-rejection; the nature of lightness is self-acceptance.*

To Do

Once you experience how light you can be about your life, you will have both courage and discipline. Courage gives you the will to initiate an action, and discipline gives you the will to carry it out. Choosing lighter is far easier than all of the effort you exert holding onto positions that avoid the light.

Love them just because you do, not for what they can do, have done, or promise to do.

Get up tomorrow looking for success in your day.

Go to bed tonight appreciating one item that you have in your life.

Share with someone five items that you wish someone else would share with you.

Take on an extra project at work just because you know it needs to be done.

Volunteer to help a friend without having them sign an "I.O.U."

A fundamental misunderstanding about

Choosing

is that you shouldn't choose for yourself.

Waking up from a deep sleep will always present you with choices, and you will want a way to make choices that will prove true to you. Your choices will not betray you when you think big about them, when you stretch yourself enough to discover lightness.

Sometimes good fortune is on your side, and the choices you make turn out fine. They bring relief, success, and do no harm anywhere. Those choices are not a problem. It's the choices you make that are a burden, the ones that create helpless and hopeless, or encompass your life in heaviness that are the trouble.

When you make choices that leave you feeling down about yourself, think about why you make those choices. You make them for various reasons, but you always want them to get you something.

A Matter of Choice

—You make them because you are angry, and you want to prove your point.

—You make them because you expect someone will compensate you.

—You make them because you want what you don't have.

—You make them because you believe they owe you something.

—You make them because you have expectations about a fixed outcome.

—You make them because you want to be happy, and you believe your choice will guarantee happiness.

—You make them because you believe you have no other recourse but the one choice that is obvious.

—And you make them to get where you fantasize that happiness lives.

When such choices don't get you what you want, it might be because you haven't clearly defined what that is. Often you make choices to satisfy one part of yourself, only to discover that they brought uneasiness to another part of yourself. If the effect of that uneasiness makes your original choice not worth your effort, you may become insecure about all choices, which will compound the heaviness you feel.

Just ask yourself why you make choices that leave you feeling wretched. When you make choices that you don't like, don't blame the process. The choice is usually delivering a message to you. Sometimes the message is a gentle warning, asking you to look where you haven't, look where you won't, or not to look where you are. Other times you cannot see the obvious choice that will lighten you because you earlier made a decision not to look for or to feel about it the very way it would lighten you. Just don't quit too soon. Stay in the situation while you continue to see the same thing. Maybe all you need to do is to think a new way about the old agenda. Decide to make your choices from a larger premise concerning your life.

Choices

Discomfort does not exist in making the choice that lightens; it exists before you discover the choice that lightens. Choice that brings lightness does not play tricks on you. The very experience of lightness illuminates, making your encounters easier and brighter. The load of your life becomes less severe and less harsh. The choice that lightens has a delicate yet powerful impact.

Your need to manipulate your life limits your ability to put your trust in choices that lighten you. If you make choices that aren't true to you, you will get another opportunity. For choices ultimately work to align you in response to your inner plea for lightness.

When you experience scarcity of lightness, make another choice, one that brings you closer to lightness. Because once you have the experience, you will know what is true for you. You can set down your expectations, your anger, and your blame. Burden is dark and heavy, and it does not exist in the same space with light. When you choose the light, you will feel light, you will be lighter, and others in your life will experience this lightness.

So lighten up, and play a game with choices. Try a few on, and see how they feel. Do they lighten you? Look for the hidden choice. Sometimes the very choice that will lighten the situation hides from you while it continues to seduce you.

Don't be afraid to choose and, if you are afraid, choose anyway. Keep in mind that you are looking for the silver lining—the light behind the darkness. It is always there waiting patiently for you to access it. There is no scarcity of lightness.

The nature of not choosing is heaviness; the nature of choosing is feeling lighter.

To Do

When you look for choices that give you a way out, you are limiting your choices. Look for those choices that give you the way into or straight through, and you will experience an abundance of choices.

Treat yourself as well as you would a lover.

Think that they do love you and start gathering evidence to prove it.

Believe that it will work out, and look for ways to make that happen.

Decide not to quit until you quit.

Make a list of every choice you can think of. Add ten more choices to your list—add ten more choices to your list—until you uncover the lighter choice.

Forgive them rather than accuse them.

Find the compromise that makes everyone happy.

Choose not to think "Shame on them," or "Shame on me."

Give them one more chance, and point out their successes.

Choose a day next week to be happy all day.

A fundamental misunderstanding about

Waking Up

is that nothing happens while you are asleep.

Sometimes people do the motions of living, just getting to the end of each day, never thinking about life and what is happening about their living. Perhaps they forget as the days go by that the only life they have is living itself. It is easy to get caught up in the habits of living and to forget that there is only so much time to live a life by choice.

Sometimes years pass before they begin to wonder where the time has gone. Suddenly, the kids are grown, or it's time to retire, or they remember it was just yesterday that they were dreaming dreams about their potential. When they do begin to wonder about the turn of events of their life, they may feel as if they have missed something, as if something happened without their knowledge. A sense of panic envelopes people when they consider that years have passed, and they weren't ready.

Life does not wait for anyone while it is passing. It continues moment to moment, whether you are depressed or happy, satisfied or discontent, young or old, ready or not. Living is more than just getting by. While you are busy manipulating time so it cooperates with your schedule, what pieces of life are you saying no to?

—Have you forgotten that life does not owe you? Do you quit your life when your desires are not fulfilled just as you planned?

—Have you forgotten that today is one day of your life and you want something from it? Or are you often glad the day is over because everything that could go wrong did?

—Have you forgotten that there are just so many days of your life to live and that soon it will be over? Is it too painful or unsatisfying to experience the condition of your life so you ignore it and hope for better days?

—Have you forgotten that you have choices about the experiences of your life? Or do you feel as if bad things have always happened to you, and you are used to it?

—Have you forgotten that your right to living includes the right to make your days count in your favor? How many days of the life you planned and have lived can you count as great days?

—Have you forgotten that most people won't care if you live each day as much as you will? They are busy trying to get through their own life, and they will hardly notice your's. In fact, others tend to use you and abuse you when you sleep through your life. Abuse is an alarm trying to wake you up.

Perhaps you are making plans for the future and living in a state of, "I plan to do thus and so when other things are settled." Are you waiting for life to get positioned perfectly before you go on with it? "When the kids grow up, I will have the career I want; when we get a large enough bank account, we will have children; after I pay for their college education, I will quit this job and have the business I always wanted; when I'm no longer responsible for my parents, we will take that dream trip; when they retire, I will have the job I want; after Christmas, I'll get a divorce."

You can find many reasons to sleep through life and wait for the life you always wanted to show up, but what is so important that you find yourself denying life right now? The problem with waiting to live life is that it is still going on while you are waiting. You will wake up some morning and realize you are in the same state of waiting that you were in ten years ago. The only thing that has changed is that you are ten years older and ten years less courageous. To live the days of life requires that you live them awake; then you will find that each day has something in it especially for you. When you are awake, you get to have choices about your life.

Choices

Living fully depends upon your ability to stay awake and participate in your life; living awake is a full time proposition. Practice being awake when you are awake. Many events occur about which you will want to make choices in your best interest.

Making choices for the moment is more challenging than it may seem. You must live and be in the moment to recognize your many choices. Life presents you with all of the things you could want or need, when you stay awake and make choices for the moment you are living. When you think about your choices, think that the effective ones are about your life, right now, this moment. You cannot relive the past, and you cannot live in the future. When you see this, you will see how few of the usual decisions you do make have to do with the moment you are living right now. Your mind tends rather to make decisions to insure a future outcome or to prevent a recurrence of a past event. And that is what limits your choices.

—Your mind often believes your choices are limited. If you tend to make choices based on expectations of the outcome, your choices do seem limited. The scenario is that you can't make X choice because this will happen and you can't make Y choice because that will happen.

—Because life presents you with so many choices and you are making it up that you only have a few, you are sometimes confused about what should happen in your life. It may be in your best interest to make the choice to give up and give in. It may be in your best interest to move on and move out. But whatever choice you make, make it from good will for everyone concerned. Hold the idea of "I want for me, and I want for you."

—One notion about your choices is that others won't like the ones you make. They won't like it if you change careers or take up a hobby that nourishes you. However, when you are in touch with your life inside, you won't make choices that terrorize others. You know that you feel best when they feel best.

—Another notion about choices is that they can't be undone—once you choose something, you must live with that choice forever. When you live by this notion you are limiting your choices. You are skipping over the moment and getting into forever with your idea.

Choices are not what get you into jams. Choices are opportunities to live your life from the inside out. Without choices you are limited to waiting for something to happen on the outside so that you can react rather than choose. Remember that your life happens on the inside when you are awake and making choices, and then you manifest it on the outside. And you will want to make choices that lighten you on the inside.

> *The nature of asleep is done to;*
> *the nature of awake is in charge.*

To Do

Asleep is a state of the mind. Your mind wants to sleep rather than be present having to cope. It seems easier to be asleep and excuse your problems with, "I didn't know." However, the more you stay awake and notice, the fewer accidents have an opportunity to happen.

Stay awake the next time you don't like how things are going.

Do the things you don't like to do better than you did them last time.

Tomorrow, give up resentments.

Choose not to participate the next time the same old argument comes up.

Choose to support your boss.

Choose to tackle some of your hard things.

Choose to think well of yourself today.

A fundamental misunderstanding about

Taking Charge

is that you can't.

Things happen. Sometimes you may wonder why they happen, and especially to you. You are just living your life, and things are going along, and then, in a moment, something happens. Something you don't like. Something you certainly wouldn't choose. Something you didn't ask for, and you don't want.

Or perhaps over a period of time, you notice that something is happening. At first you ignore it, thinking that it will go away. But it keeps showing up until one day, you find yourself face to face with it—the very last thing that you may have wanted.

—You are going along living your life, and although your relationship has been showing signs of difficulty, you thought that was only a phase. And then one day, they come home and say they have had an affair.

—Or you have been at your job for years, and although you have not received the promotions you desired and the evaluations you feel you deserved, nevertheless it was a secure job. And then one day, you receive word that your services are no longer required.

—Or you are driving along in rush hour traffic, listening to the radio, anxious for dinner, when someone loses control of their car, and you are in their accident.

—Or you visit your doctor for a routine visit, and although you know that you really haven't been quite well for awhile now, you are advised that you need major surgery.

—Or someone you love very much dies. Perhaps they die suddenly, or perhaps they die after a long and painful illness. But no matter what their age or the circumstances, they are gone.

When something happens, you find yourself trying to understand it. You ask, "Why did this happen to me? What did I do to deserve this?" Often you may feel like the victim of life itself—like a billiard ball randomly bouncing from event to event, sustaining gaping wounds and massive bruises, feeling done-to.

You will find yourself trying to find a way to think about it.

—You may think that it is the worst thing that ever happened to you. You are sure that it has ruined your life. You cannot go on living given this state of affairs. There is no point.

—Or you may think that, if nothing else, if you survive this one, you will have learned much. Experience is the greatest teacher, and this teacher just arrived in your life.

—Or maybe you can think that it may be the best thing. For a moment you view the event and realize that you can't really see the long-term outcome, but no matter how devastated you are at this moment, there must be a silver lining somewhere.

Sometimes when bad things happen, you simply feel stuck. You don't know how to feel. Sometimes you are so depressed about them that you can't get out of bed. Sometimes you forget about them totally, even for a few moments, and find some peace. Or sometimes, as you share the content with others and begin to hear their opinions and judgments, you find yourself carrying around so many positions that you picked up from other people that you don't know what to think. And sometimes, you are so stuck that you feel you can't decide anything at all. The only option is to continue to let the events bounce around until finally, at some point, they settle, and then perhaps you will know what to think.

Choices

When you find yourself in a happening that you can't change the content of, you may wonder what choices you have. There are ways to tell.

—Some of the choices you make imprison you. They build walls around you so high that you can't see the light that is dawning all about you. If you choose a position of hopeless, then hopeless is what you get.

—Some of the choices you make depress you. You become immobilized with feelings of helplessness. If you choose depression, then you are depressed.

—And some of the choices you make set you free. They can't change the content, but they do change how you hold the content. And that changes your experience of the content.

When you are facing infidelity, for example, there are many positions that you can have. One position is that you will get a divorce and get them in the process, for they have betrayed you. One position is that you will get a divorce, and that you will part friends, knowing that life's pathways sometimes take people in different directions.

Or again, if you are fired, you may choose to recognize that even though there is present anxiety involved, this event may open doors that otherwise you would have refused to open. No matter what content shows up, even as you experience the first moments of anger and pain, there might be a small voice in the background reminding you that the perfect job is just around the corner, if you are willing to look.

When something happens, remind yourself that you are at choice about your experience of it, about your handling of it, about the position you will take about it. You will want to look at all your options, and choose a position that lightens the experience for you. Hold it in a way that enhances your living your life, that doesn't immobilize you, that doesn't victimize you.

Of course you have to live through whatever it is, but staying trapped in initial positions of depression, pain, anger, rage, hopelessness will not enhance your experience. These positions, in fact, only add to the depression, pain, anger, rage, and hopelessness that the happening itself brought.

You will not want to live the experience hundreds of times over. You will want to look for a position that will enable you to move ahead, through the immediate pain and anger, and into a life where the event is past tense. You know that time heals all things. But you can decide how much time. Do you want to wait forever; for ten years; for ten months?

When something happens, pick a position as soon as you can. You want to decide how you are going to be in the situation, how you are going to hold the situation, how you are going to feel. You want to know that, even if you can't reach the rainbow in the next moment, that is where you are heading.

Consider looking at situations objectively. Stand back from pain and anger and say to yourself, if only for a moment, "Isn't this interesting? I wonder what choices I have. I wonder what choices I want to make." You may want to choose never to let the situation go below "interesting" in your mind. Decide never to plunge into despair—that the lowest you will allow yourself to experience the event is at "interesting." If you are able to take one step away from the immediacy of the event, you will be able to see possibilities; possibilities that are in your best interest, possibilities that will facilitate your living through the worst, possibilities that will enhance your experience of the happening.

> *The nature of being happened to*
> *is victimhood;*
> *the nature of living the happening*
> *as you choose is control.*

To Do

The more you are able to look at your world and see what you do have, what your choices are, what positions you can take, how you can experience your life, the lighter your life will be. You cannot always pick the happenings that arrive in your life. You can choose how you will receive and hold them. You want to choose positions that enable you to live the content as you choose.

Look for a different way to experience a happening that always happens to you.

Catch the happening at the beginning, and choose how you want to experience it.

Look for the larger meaning that the happening brings.

Remember that no matter how it looks at the moment, it will change.

Look for the challenge of the happening, and choose a different response.

Choose to deal with it sooner rather than later.

Choose not to make it more serious than it is.

Choose to keep it to yourself.

Be glad some things happen.

A fundamental misunderstanding about

Selfishness

is that loving yourself means you are selfish.

When you love someone, they are a primary consideration in your life. Sometimes you sacrifice for them, ignoring your personal desires to ensure that they will be happy and content. Other times your loving them means that you will be particular ways with them and do certain things for them. And of course you will do your best to fulfill their needs and wishes. You will feel sad for their hurts; you will feel glad for their accomplishments. You will treat them as if they are your very best friend, and you wouldn't want to betray them.

When you think about loving someone that way, did it ever occur to you to think about loving yourself? Or are you afraid that thinking about loving yourself will require that you love your other, your children, your siblings, your parents, or your friends less?

Maybe you believe that it is more important to satisfy someone else's needs before considering your own. Do you believe that loving them and caring for their desires is more important than caring for yourself? If you have experienced these situations, you may want to think about how you think about you.

—Maybe you think that you can't love yourself because you've made too many mistakes.

—Or you can't love yourself because you heard them when they said you were unlovable.

—You can't love yourself because you learned it was egotistical.

—You can't love yourself because you don't live up to your expectations.

—You can't love yourself because you aren't anyone special.

—You can't love yourself because you are afraid you will fail.

—You can't love yourself because you don't even know yourself.

—You can't love yourself because you are you own worst critic.

—You can't love yourself because your family wouldn't like you anymore.

—You can't love yourself because you never considered it.

Fortunately there is a friend waiting for your attention. Someone who will care if you love them, and someone who will succeed with your encouragement. This person has wanted to be your first consideration your whole life. And this person will continue to improve their life with your support and goodwill. When no one else will love you, this person will be on your side. This person will never leave you, and if you treat this person kindly, there is no end to the rewards you will receive. When you consider loving someone, consider loving your *self* first.

Choices

Some times self-love is thought of as narcissistic. It is frowned upon and seen as vanity or selfishness, as egocentricity or self-centeredness. People are warned about the dangers of loving themselves.

There is a vast difference between loving yourself as your first consideration and deriving erotic gratification from the admiration of your physical or mental attributes. When you love yourself you give validity to your needs and wishes. You give credence to your personal right to live happy and fulfilled. Loving yourself carries a commitment to providing an atmosphere that enhances your well-being.

Loving yourself means caring and thinking about your life and what you want to accomplish living your life. You will be your best friend and treat yourself with gentleness. You will have compassion for your mistakes, and you will nourish yourself when you feel empty.

When you love yourself, you will experience a greater capacity to love others. Loving them will bring no expectations because you are capable of understanding their humanness. After all, you love yourself; therefore you understand just what it means to be alive. You know that loving yourself is not selfish. It is just a fact that you cannot care about another, be more concerned for another, consider them or love them more than you do yourself, because loving begins with you.

> *The nature of self-denial is bitterness;*
> *the nature of self-love is joy.*

To Do

Loving yourself manifests in many ways, and it has many rewards. When you love yourself, you critique yourself for the purpose of learning, not punishing. You are gentle in your thoughts about what you have done, what you are doing, and what you want to do. You notice your achievements and do more of those things that make you feel worthwhile. You don't abuse yourself, and you don't allow others to abuse you. You think highly of yourself, and you care what you think. You will experience rewards loving yourself just as you experience rewards in loving another.

Put a note in your pocket that says you are OK.

Criticize yourself only with the purpose of teaching.

Reconsider having conversations with others where you tell them everything that is wrong with you.

Do two things that you have always wanted to do for yourself.

When you wake up, think about what you will do today that makes you feel good about yourself.

Compliment yourself when you deserve it.

Get your opinion of yourself from yourself.

Give yourself permission to play and have fun.

Be your own best advisor.

Have compassion for you.

*A
fundamental
misunderstanding
about*

Change

*is that if
things change
they will be
better or worse.*

Change is one of those topics that many people are ambivalent about. Some people resist change because of personal encounters with it or because they have witnessed another's encounter with it. For others, it is difficult to appreciate the benefits of change because they remember only that they were required to experience their drama of living when change made its appearance.

So change sometimes is categorized as an ominous feeling that occasionally surfaces to remind you that life has surprises. Perhaps you have enough surprises planned and that is all you desire to cope with. Also, you know that change can trigger that nervous feeling that makes you believe that you can't depend upon tomorrow.

Besides, you have it all arranged so you can sleep through tomorrow and everything will continue in just the same manner. If you inadvertently experience or witness the insecurity of your life reorganizing itself, you may feel an urgency to get things settled once again. You want confirmation that people and situations will be reliable; maybe then you can relax into the pseudo-experience that you call life.

It is a small and comfortably familiar world that you nestle yourself into. You move through life much the same every day, and you hardly notice that things are changing as you grow older. It is change that makes the energy of life move, even if it does seem to threaten the artificial security that you have come to depend on. You expect others to behave and events to unfold within a prescribed format and within predictable dimensions. If something happens outside of the standard dimension, it threatens your illusion of security.

Did you realize that resistance to change is grounded in the same insecurity that you believe change creates? That may be why change is so resisted.

—Maybe change is blamed for discomfort in your life.

—Maybe you believe they can count on you if things don't change.

—Maybe you believe you will know what to do and how to be if things don't change.

—Maybe you think you will have security and peace if things don't change.

—Maybe you believe you can master the situation if things don't change.

—Maybe you believe things will turn out better if you can get it down the way it is now.

—Maybe you believe you won't have to work so hard if things stay the same.

—Maybe you know that you would just get through your life, planning your laughs and planning your sorrows, if nothing ever changed.

—Maybe you believe you will have control if nothing changes.

—Maybe you believe you will have to make decisions that you feel unqualified to make if things change.

—Maybe you can't always get life to be fair if things keep changing.

While you are thinking these thoughts, people and situations are changing right before you. Resisting or denying change doesn't seem to have any effect. Since it happens no matter what, you might want to review your relationship to change. Even if you are not noticing, things are changing. With all of this change happening about you, you may wonder what you can count on. Why does change occur?

Choices

When you decide to embrace change, it can be your ally. Change is not out to disturb you—it is there to remind you that you are alive. If you embraced change, you would know exactly how to behave about your life. Change is the element about life that asks you to stretch yourself until you get out of breath. It brings character and light to an otherwise bland experience.

—Change brings with it an opportunity for new experiences to assure you that you will continue to live in your life.

—Change brings an opportunity of discovery about yourself that increases your ability to fulfill your potential.

—Change brings with it opportunities to live in a manner that opens new avenues of expertise to you.

—Change assists you knowingly or unknowingly in your efforts to reach your destiny.

—Change is a natural event of life that happens quietly and progressively when you have no resistance.

—Change restores balance where there is distress and dis-ease.

Change is at once gentle, compelling, and demanding. It will invite you to take stock of your life and to revise those things that are no longer in your best interest. Or it will draw your attention and you will invite it, hoping it will act as a medium to help you escape the unpleasantness of your present experience. However change occurs, you can count on the fact that it is happening.

You can't outfox change. It happens with or without your participation. It happens all around you while you are waiting to take part in life.

> *The nature of resistance is staying stuck;*
> *the nature of change is movement.*

To Do

Your very best option concerning change is to welcome it. There is a natural security in knowing that things will change. Live your life looking forward to the experience that change promises you. Look forward to each day with wonderment knowing that this day things are changing. Discover what is new about the life you are living today. Change is not your enemy; your struggle comes from resisting change.

Real living will necessitate your surrender to change. Then you will discover a sense of peace and security because you will have it settled. You have settled on change.

Change the way you think before you change the situation.

Change how you talk about yourself.

Change how you speak to your kids.

Drive a new route to work.

Stay at your desk for lunch.

Change how you feel about doing your job.

Change your mind about rejecting them.

Change your attitude about who is right and who is wrong.

*A
fundamental
misunderstanding
about*

Risk

> *is that
> risk
> is a negative
> proposition.*

The word "security" brings up all kinds of feelings for some people. Some are angry because they have security and others are angry because they don't. Depending upon your definition of security, you may or may not possess it at any given moment.

Security is elusive in that sometimes you have it concerning a particular item and the next moment you don't. When you think about it, every item of content in your life can be secure or not. Your relationship can be secure, your job can be secure, and your financial status can be secure, or not.

Some believe if they follow all of the rules exactly, they will achieve security shortly. It lives just around the bend from getting the right experience, the right credentials, the right relationship, the right therapist. Maybe you have lived most of your life chasing security, and you believe you have achieved it. Very often it escapes you as soon as you achieve it, or you are not happy now that you have it.

Security is one of those issues that doesn't seem to cooperate just because you want it to. And it is only an issue for you when it is an issue; it isn't an issue until it is threatened. You lose your job, they unexpectedly ask for a divorce, the kids don't turn out, or the stock market doesn't cooperate.

When security is an issue, it can be a major issue. You may feel as if your world has turned upside down. Your thoughts may be consumed with ways to regain it. Why did you lose it, and when will you get it again? When feelings about lost security accelerate, they can be like a nightmare because now you might have to risk some part of yourself in pursuit of it.

—You might have to risk some of the beliefs that you hold so dear.

—You might have to risk understanding because every rule you gathered to insure security has been shattered.

—You might have to risk your way of life because the same life patterns are no longer applicable to your present situation. The solutions you have lived with no longer work, and the ideas that have always gotten you through are obsolete.

When this happens in your life you can make the choice to embrace risk. You will want to anyway because the paradox is that living to insure security is risky—you may get the security that you have struggled to achieve and discover that you created very little life to live; and living without security is risky.

Choices

It is not ever difficult to discover where and when risk is seducing you. It is present in your life. Look where you are bored, where you are frustrated, where you are disabled, where you are unsatisfied. Risk asks you to make choices about the present circumstance without insurance about the outcome. You may have to make decisions in the moment without your mind reprimanding and reminding you of past mistakes or pain.

Your mind wants you to avoid risk because it has a lot of proof that similar decisions caused anguish. You can rely on your mind to trash almost any experience of risk when you have made some difficult and challenging decision. Your mind doesn't know the difference between what did hurt and what might hurt, and it wants to protect you against any real or imagined pain.

You may have to live parts of your life without checking out with your mind what it thinks about the risk you are about to take. You may have to live each moment answering to your inner self and deciding to follow your dreams or not. The choice is yours. Taking risk is not as unsettling as it may seem. When you think about the large idea of life, you begin to realize that there is no real security anyway. To live your life to achieve security has a false reality attached to it. You are living a reality that is extremely fragile. That reality leads to a life of fixed life experience. You are creating an illusion that has the potential to be shattered the moment some character gets out of place. And it is not hard to see that characters living or imagined can't be manipulated by your ideas of security.

But when you do choose to risk and follow your dreams, it will bring you more satisfaction and success than your mind could ever think to. You will have a life that you love to live because there is really no pain in risk. Risk does not feel so overwhelming when you are loving what you are doing and loving where you are being. Risk brings personal progress, personal challenge, and personal satisfaction to your life.

> *The nature of security is limits;*
> *the nature of risk is limitless.*

To Do

It's your inner self that will ask you to risk. And the amazing part is that the only real risk is in going in opposition to what your mind has determined to be secure. Try a few risks—the ones that your inner self has given you hints about.

Rethink your position about one thing that you wanted to do but didn't because you were advised that it was too risky.

Take one risk that you have always wanted, without making a mental list dooming your efforts.

Risk something tomorrow in the genre of self-worth.

Risk something tonight in the genre of relationship.

Risk something next Tuesday in the genre of career.

*A
fundamental
misunderstanding
about*

Communication

*is that what
you communicated
is what
you meant.*

Communication is so powerful that it influences your life in every way. Others form opinions and make decisions about you from your communications. Sometimes they use your communications as entertainment or examples. What you communicate can make your life in relationship happen and sometimes it prevents your life in relationship from happening.

Communication reveals so many aspects about you that you must not treat it casually. Nor should you expect others to magically sort through your communications to understand what you mean.

If you frequently find yourself misunderstood, perhaps

—you don't tell the truth when you communicate.

This is a bad habit but you haven't gotten around to giving it up.

—you want or need the approval of others so you hedge about your true nature just to win someone's approval.

—you want someone to believe you more than you believe yourself, so you color the facts about who you are, what you have done, or what you plan to do.

—you believe there will be big trouble in your life if you communicate the truth.

—you think the lie of omission will keep you in good favor with someone important to you.

—you didn't get their attention when you were communicating. You realized that their attention was on everything except you.

—you tell the item to get their sympathy, support, or any other favor you want.

—you don't really care what they think about what you are communicating.

—your motivations were to control rather than to share.

Understanding communication as your personal tool of power enables you to communicate exactly the message you want. You will communicate thoughts and ideas that translate who you are and what you are up to. You know if what you communicate got there by what is repeated to you and by the responses you get from others. When you get the responses you want and you are understood as you intend, your communication got there.

Choices

Communicate that you approve of and believe in yourself. Because others sense that you are able to approve of and believe in them as much as you approve of yourself.

Refrain from coloring the story to get sympathy. If you communicate that you cannot deal with very much, others will not expect much from you. You may not be invited to participate with them when, in fact, you really want to.

Consider the ramifications before you give your agreement, commitment, or add your opinions. Since others may be taking your word for it, you want your word to be a clear expression of your intention.

Tell the truth. It is so much easier to remember the truth. You don't need to add to and subtract from the facts or be concerned about what you told to whom.

Represent yourself and refrain from using other's accomplishments as your own.

Consider how they will respond if you purposefully communicate to upset them, control them, or confuse them. They may become upset, feel controlled, or misunderstand you. Ultimately, they may make decisions about you from those behaviors which can prevent further communication.

Use communication as a means to express your desires, your needs, and your nature. Use it to describe your life and your experiences, your hopes and your dreams.

Get their attention. Invite them to hear you. When it is important to you, it has a better chance to be important to them.

You will want to set yourself free with your communication. Give yourself space for change by telling them this is what's so now. Make your communication count. Everything you say is about you. Your demeanor, your words, your actions, and your attitudes will communicate who you say you are. Others will notice your genuineness and that will bring you special rewards.

> *The nature of misunderstanding is confusion;
> the nature of communication is impact.*

To Do

Your decision to communicate concisely will clear up many issues in your life. If you could inventory the causes of your problems, you would find misunderstanding is a root cause. Restating, redefining, and rewording what you want to say will, by necessity, require you to know yourself better. You will clear up preconceived notions that you and others have about you and the content of your life.

Think of a time someone said you said, when you didn't say that. How did you feel?

Think of a time that you said someone said, when they didn't say that. How do you think they felt?

When you first realize that they are not getting your communication, start over.

When it is vital for them to understand you, ask them to repeat what you said.

Before you begin your communication, know what you intend for them to get.

Choose not to communicate to manipulate or control.

Tell the truth as much as you know it.

Be courteous, be generous, be thoughtful, be wise with the words that form your communication.

*The
fundamental
misunderstanding
about*

Blame

> *is that
> blaming them
> makes
> you right.*

Whose fault is it when things don't go the way you planned, when someone doesn't respond to you the way you think they should, when you don't get exactly what you want, when your day gets out of control, or when others choose someone other than you to do what you wanted to do with them? Whose fault is it when accidents happen, when the unexpected shows up, or when bad things take a turn for the worse? Whose fault is it when you don't love your life, when you can hardly bear to face the day, or when you give up and give in?

It seems comforting and easy to pick out a particular person or situation to dump all the blame on. They don't understand you, they don't care about you, or they don't love you anymore. Therefore your life or this time in your life is no good. You know it would improve if they would be better or if they would just recognize your worth.

And it puzzles you that they don't recognize your worth because you have sacrificed your all for them, and you thought they would be grateful. You did it because you expected them to acknowledge your worth, and not only did they criticize you, but they expected you to do even more. So, naturally, they are the blame for your unhappiness. You are a good person and if they can't see that, they are ruining your life. It's their fault that you aren't where you want to be or that you don't have what you want to have. In fact, you have a running list of people and situations to blame for your life.

—It's their fault because they don't understand you is one of your favorites. You rationalize that you have their best interest in mind, for example, when you criticize their behavior or manipulate situations so that you are not pressed beyond your comfort zone.

—It's their fault because they don't really care about you, and you get to determine what counts, how much it counts, and how long it counts when they make overtures of caring about you.

—It's their fault because obviously they don't love you anymore and that must be why they are doing things differently these days. They must be making the moves they are making to hurt you because they know you want to keep the status quo.

—It's their fault because you have discussed with them the behavior you expect from them, and they keep doing what you don't like. How are you expected to be the way you want to be if they keep being the way you don't want them to be?

—It's their fault because they continue to do things that are not according to your plan.

—It's their fault because they won't let you talk about what you want to talk about.

—It's their fault because they manage the money.

—It's their fault because you let them make all of your decisions.

—It's their fault because they get mad if you don't.

—It's their fault because they get mad if you do.

Blaming others or the situation gives you the temporary feeling of being right, and part of you wants to be right more than it wants to be responsible. Part of you wants to get even, more than it wants to get on with it. It's a difficult proposition to rethink your positions.

Life brings with it many personal challenges, and it is just easier sometimes to put the blame on someone or something else. You or your situation would be perfect "if-only." However, occasionally all of the if-only conditions are met, and you still feel unsettled. If no one or no thing is to blame, what is the trouble? Who and/or what is responsible for the way you feel?

Choices

Fundamentally, there is no blame. They are not to blame, and you are not to blame. When you understand that the issue just is what is, then the responsibility is yours, which is not all that bad. When you are responsible for your life, for better or for worse, you are the one that gets to make the choices about it. Who could be better at deciding about your life than you? How can others really know what is in your best interest? You don't always know. Your desires are not etched in concrete. They are fluid, changing from encounter to encounter and from situation to situation.

To liberate yourself, don't blame yourself, just take responsibility. Remember, taking responsibility gives you choices. If you make one choice that doesn't enhance how you feel about your life, make another choice and give up blame. It never gets you what you want. It does, however, make people want to avoid you.

> *The nature of blame is denial;*
> *the nature of responsibility is respect.*

To Do

When you give up blame, you will be in charge, taking responsibility, making choices, and living life to the fullest.

Determine who really is to blame because it rained and ruined your picnic.

Notice yourself blaming them, and compliment them instead.

Choose not to blame them in order to make yourself look better.

Choose not to put them on the defensive, or to allow them to put you on the defensive.

Help them discover their responsibility by being responsible.

Go one entire day without indulging in blame.

A fundamental misunderstanding about

Guilt

is that it compensates for something.

It is preposterous to assume that someone or something else has the power to make you feel guilty. No one makes you feel guilty without your consent. It's your personal investment. You get more satisfaction from it for some reason than you get from the effort it will take to resolve the issue.

Guilt can be useful. Some reasons you use guilt are to excuse your behavior, to make right what you know isn't, to pretend that you care when you don't, to gain their confidence, and to pretend something is true that is not. It's your choice about guilt, and you may not want to give it up. It has gotten you through when you didn't come through, it has saved face for you, it has gotten you off the hook when you offended, and it has saved you having to do what you didn't want to do in the first place.

Notice those items that you feel guilty or regretful about. Does it seem like someone else says or does something that makes you feel guilty? Are you thinking you should be better, do more, or try harder? Are you sorry and regretful that pieces of your past were not different?

Sometimes you have choices other than to feel guilty. There are conflicting situations that seem to demand one thing from you when you can only give something else. So you end up feeling guilty. Maybe you want to have it one way and a favorite other wants to have it a different way. They apply pressure, make threats, or promise a payback. If you do it your way, you only end up feeling guilty.

—You feel guilty because you don't want to, and guilt is your way of compensating.

—You feel guilty because they convince you your way is the wrong way, and you are unable to do it their way.

—You feel guilty because you stood up for yourself and now you think it was a mistake.

—You feel guilty hoping it will make them sympathetic to your error.

—You feel guilty because you never had any intention of doing what they wanted even though you agreed.

—You feel guilty because it's a habit.

—You feel guilty hoping others will think you care.

—You feel guilty thinking that they will think you are nicer than you think you are.

—You feel guilty because you haven't done it, and they counted on you.

—You feel guilty because things didn't turn out the way you hoped.

—You feel guilty because you expect others to do what you will not do.

Guilt is often used to control and manipulate. You have a vested interest that the outcome be your way rather than their way. Other times it is used as an excuse to prolong the obvious. When you are feeling guilty or regretful it is time for you to reconsider. Did they do it to you or are you wanting to avoid what you need to do? Did you do anything to them or are you considering your life? Perhaps you are tired of the game of guilt and what it gets you?

Feeling guilty is an indication that your interior life is suffering. It wants you to take another look at the particular situation. It wants you to begin anew. It is telling you there is another chance to be honest with your *self* and to make it right with you.

A Matter of Choice

Choices

The fabric of guilt is self-doubt and manipulation. Guilt and regret are the other side of wishing and hoping. You wish or hope that the other would or wouldn't, or that the situation had been or will be.

If you are tired of living with guilt, you will need to take some action. You can accomplish so much more when you are not using your energy to feel guilty. Use your energy to do the best you can, and don't look back. Looking back won't change it, and tomorrow is another chance to use your energy the way you want. Do what you intend to, and don't promise to do that which you don't intend to do.

> *The nature of guilt is thwarted intention;*
> *the nature of guiltless is self-assured.*

To Do

You have the power to clear up those items that you feel guilty about by doing what you really intend to do and by not pretending to do those things that you don't intend to do. Removing guilt begins with being honest with yourself. You can only do your best and then allow it to turn out the way it does. Do your best, and what happens will happen. When you no longer doubt yourself, you will no longer feel guilty.

Only say you will do what you will do.

Choose not to use guilt as an excuse.

Finish that one project that you feel most guilty about.

Admit that you won't do it when you know you won't.

Say yes to those requests that are appropriate for you.

Fix what you can fix.

*A
fundamental
misunderstanding
about*

Worry

*is
that
you
have to.*

Doesn't it sometimes seem strange the items you find yourself worried about? You worry about items that directly affect your life, and you worry about items that have little to do with you. You worry about the stranger that you thought seemed unhappy, the stray dog that you saw on the street, the child walking home from the park, the weather report on television, jobs, loves, children, money, sex, war, peace, and health. If you kept a log, how much of your time would you find consumed with thoughts that worry you?

Maybe your mind has little to think about if it is not worried, so it looks for items to worry about. Maybe you realize things just aren't normal if you aren't worried about something, so you even worry that you aren't worried, or you worry about what they are thinking about what you are telling them you are worried about. You can worry so much that when you come to a solution about what you were worried about, you might worry yourself right past it. Once it starts, it seems like there's no end to it.

—Worry can ruin your free time. You go on vacation and you are so worried about what is going on where you are not, that the whole time where you are is ruined.

—Worry can also make good times turn sour. Your lifetime dream just came true, so now you worry about not having a dream or how you will keep it now that you have it.

—Worry can be an facade to make people think you are concerned. Maybe you have pretended worry so much that now you are actually worried.

Sometimes people realize how you worry so they use worry to control you. They don't show up as agreed, and you worry. They know that; it puts them in charge. Maybe you need to find other ways to let them know you love them.

Behind the energy of worry is your desire to control. You believe the more you can control life, the less you will have to worry. Consider whether you want to continue to use your precious energy letting your mind find things to worry about. If you give your mind permission to worry, then worry will take up all your thoughts and all your time.

Worry is the way you expend your energy rather than doing something to settle the situation. It seems easier to worry than to do what needs to be done. It seems easier to worry than to say what needs to be said.

Choices

Some items you really are concerned about. You will notice that when you have a genuine concern you begin to find solutions, or you use the energy of your concern to help the situation where you can. The difference is that you want to get to resolution of the issue, and you direct your energy in the appropriate manner. You do not feel hopeless or helpless, controlled or controlling. You get yourself moving in some direction, doing something.

Worry is a process of the mind, whereas concern is a process of action. When you are worried, you will find your mind rehashing the current details, and throwing in a few you weren't thinking about previously. The real trouble with worrying is that it will produce evidence for its case. If you look for evidence that you should worry, you will probably find it. You may want to make your life easier, when you find yourself worried, by asking "What is the concern here, and what can I do?"

> *The nature of worry is control;*
> *the nature of concern is caring.*

To Do

Indulging in worry is an exercise. It pacifies your mind about items you can't or won't do anything about. If you want the jangled nerves of worry to ease, look for what you can do with your energy of concern.

Spend less, or make more, but relax about money.

Do something that you know you need to do to maintain good health.

Keep in contact with someone you worry about.

Consider whether it has happened yet before you worry about it.

Make it right with them when you are at fault.

*A
fundamental
misunderstanding
about*

Fear

*is that
limiting your experiences
prevents you
from being afraid.*

Fear is an emotion that many people avidly try to avoid. Their avoidance insidiously influences their lives by limiting their willingness to experience and to make decisions. They meticulously arrange their lives wanting to determine the outcome of each experience. Sometimes their fear is warranted; more often, its origin is vague and mysterious.

Notice that the message that fear often brings with it is about how you are limiting your life by limiting the experience of your life. Sometimes you avoid the obvious experience or avoid making the obvious decision, hoping to control your experience and dissipate the fear.

—Are you afraid of change? Do you keep the status quo, when you know it's time to move on?

—Are you afraid you will look foolish if you don't live up to the challenge, so you don't try?

—Are you afraid of making decisions, and you wonder why you feel stuck?

—Are you afraid you aren't good enough, yet you know you are doing your personal best?

—Are you afraid of the outcome if you do what you need and want?

—Are you afraid of what they will think when you honestly give your input?

—Are you afraid you will dissolve into emotion if you face new situations?

—Are you afraid you can't deal with it if you remove yourself from unhealthy situations?

—Are you afraid of conclusions others will make about you if they really knew you?

Fear of experience is a debilitating emotion. Many times the effort it requires to avoid an experience is so exhausting, with its consuming demand for your attention, that it actually creates the fear. If you find yourself thinking you can't or you won't or you shouldn't or you never, you may want to examine the nature of your beliefs.

Choices

Can you remember a time that you could no longer control the situation and were thrust into the experience of facing what you feared? You may have learned that the way to actually deal with your fears is to confront them; that requires you to experience your life.

What is it about your life that you know needs to move or expand? How do you avoid moving or expanding your experience? What do you hope to accomplish by avoiding the experience?

Think of some of the items you fear, and notice how you have arranged your life to avoid facing the emotion of fear. Fear never goes away by avoiding it. It goes away when it is not grounded by your agreement with it. Notice the many ways that you agree with your fear. You can't, won't, shouldn't, or never because you don't want to face the fear.

LET IT GO!

To get beyond the grip of fear requires your determination to experience your life in spite of your fear. Do it anyway. Fear immobilizes you when you believe you must live in a way that won't produce fear. Even if you have found a way to live where you never experience fear, can you actually call it living?

A Matter of Choice

> *The nature of fear is control;*
> *the nature of living is experience.*

To Do

You may have some fears but you are not your fears. Fear cannot control you unless you cooperate with it. To overcome fears that limit you requires that you do it in spite of your fear.

When you are afraid of what might happen, distract yourself until it happens. Notice if it actually happens.

When you would like to have the experience, choose not to use the excuse that you can't because you are afraid.

When fear is pursuing you, call a friend and talk about something else.

Make a decision to stop telling others that you are afraid.

Dwell on your successes.

Do one thing that you are afraid of doing.

*A
fundamental
misunderstanding
about*

Approval

*is that your
pointing out
where they are wrong
empowers them.*

One unfortunate assumption about relating is that you know what is best for another. Your particular belief systems convince you that you are the authority about the best way, the right way, the only way. The nuisance of being an authority is the implication that you must take action to enforce obedience.

—You think you know best because you have been there and now you know better.

—You think you know best because you have learned the right way.

—You think you know best because you have always had that opinion.

—You think you know best because your position has given you some power.

—You think you know best because so many others agree with you.

—You think you know best because you have standards.

—You think you know best because they are wrong.

You believe they have the potential to meet your expectations, and you feel justified in being the taskmaster of their lives. If occasionally you throw in an approval, you know it is only an occasional approval because most people cannot, will not, and don't live up to your standards.

When you find others resisting your critiques, you may need to think more about approval. Approval is the key that will remove the thankless burden of being taskmaster. Once you approve, you become free to enjoy your own life and the lives of others.

Choices

It is never difficult for people to feel bad about themselves. Feelings of "wrong," " bad," " inappropriate," " unworthy," "unsuccessful" are primary thoughts for many. Often it only takes a trivial comment to trigger the myriad of feelings that keep self-esteem at its lowest ebb.

A commitment to approving of yourself and others can be an empowering decision toward stamping out the wrongness of life. Choose to monitor your thoughts and divert them before you make those throw-away comments that support wrongness. When you make this commitment, you will champion approval.

Your children, parents, colleagues, employees, lovers, and friends want to be OK with you. If you want them to listen to your input, find a way to comment about them that they are able to hear. They have ears that will turn you off if they realize that what you do mostly is find fault. However, they will respond to gentle criticism born of approval. Both you and they know if you actually approve. Empower them by intending that your comments enhance their life.

> *The nature of wrong promotes resistance; the nature of approval promotes cooperation.*

To Do

Approval is a luxury to many people. You can be of great influence in others' lives when you are generous with approval. It is never difficult to find items you can approve of. When you are looking for the best in yourself or others, you naturally find it.

Approve of one item about your most difficult person, and tell it to them.

Look for what they do right all day tomorrow.

Rather than tell them what is the best way for them to be, ask them how they are.

Find three ways to express your approval of your family.

Notice your throw-away disapproval of your children, your significant other, your boss. Throw it away.

Empower one person this week with your genuine approval.

Majorly think approval.

*A
fundamental
misunderstanding
about*

Trust

*is that
someone believes
when you think
they should.*

It is foolish to assume that simply being in relationship creates the atmosphere of trust or belief. There are times in your relationships that you expect another to believe you because you have prepared your alibi. That is when you cover up to get them to believe what you want rather than what is true.

Other times you want them to cooperate, so you do or say whatever you need to get that to happen. And maybe you don't want to deal with their drama so you say or do what you think will keep them happy.

Have you ever elaborately planned the believable story? The one that leaves nothing to question or chance. The one where nothing could go wrong. And then they don't believe you. Did you wonder what went wrong? Why did they question you? Why didn't they believe you? Well, maybe

—they don't believe you because you don't believe you.

—they don't believe you because you have told too many versions of the same story.

—they don't believe you because you are telling them what you think they want to hear.

—they don't believe you because you can't face them when you say it.

—they don't believe you because what you say is impossible.

—they don't believe you because you say one thing and then do the opposite.

—they don't believe you because you project suspicion.

—they don't believe you because they know you have hidden investments in your story.

Maybe you keep telling them you love how they are, yet you continually criticize them. You can always point out their faults, or you can improve on what they have accomplished, or you can add to what they think.

Do they believe you love them? Do you love them, or do you love what you want them to be? Have you told them you wanted to be with them more than anything else and at the last minute made some excuse to cancel your date with them? Should they believe they are the most important to you?

Choices

Belief is the element that creates trust. The idea of trust poses questions like "Why should they trust you, what should they trust you to do, when should they trust you?" If you suddenly realize they don't believe you about trivial items, it may be that what you have been telling them is not the same as what you have been up to. They will only believe you to the extent that your actions are the same as what you want them to believe. Belief is only an issue when you are trying to make something so that is not so.

The bigger the issue of belief the harder it will be to establish if it is not true. Belief has a natural energy that makes your interactions with others sincere. If the natural energy is not there, nothing you can do will convince them. They know when to believe you.

Belief lives inside of you, not within them. They believe or not and you believe or not based on your experiences of relating with each other. You cannot make them believe you one way or the other. Belief doesn't need proof or evidence. When your motivations are the same as your actions, they will believe you.

> *The nature of disbelief is suspicion;
> the nature of belief is trust.*

To Do

Trust originates inside of you and when it is evident, they will believe you. Trust puts you into relationship with yourself, helping you maintain the integrity of other loving relationships.

Tell them that what is true is true for you now.

If you feel a lie coming on, ask them to give you time to think about it.

Be reliable; keep your commitments.

If you have to tell them to maintain your integrity, be prepared to accept their reaction.

Only claim it's true if you know it is.

Be honest with yourself all day.

*A
fundamental
misunderstanding
about*

Perfect

*is that
there is
one right way
to do and be.*

Have you ever wondered why you can't find the right formula, the right book, the right instructions, the right direction to help you make the perfect decisions about living? Your search for rights has led you in different directions and has created many changes in your life. You want to raise your kids the right way, find the right job, belong to the right religion, have the right house, do the right thing, get the right relationship, and set the right goals. Actually, you want to be and do perfectly—no mistakes, no room for error, and no room for growth or change. There are many reasons you want it to be perfect, and there are ways you manipulate it to get it to be perfect.

—You want to be perfect yourself because you hate others to criticize you.

—You want your kids to be perfect so that they will believe you are a great parent, even though you secretly believe you don't have enough experience about kids.

—You want the perfect job, so that you can relax and not have to worry.

—You want the perfect relationship so that you don't have to exert yourself when you are in a bad mood.

—You want the perfect home so that others will believe you are on top of it.

—You want the perfect friends so that others will be impressed with the names in your address book.

—You want the perfect look so that others will know you are successful.

You can spend a lot of valuable energy manipulating your life to make your content, yourself, and others fit your idea of perfect. Maybe even, for awhile, you can believe that you have found the perfect formula. All you have to do is keep the formula functional, and all will be well. Suddenly, without warning, subtle signs begin to present themselves that all is not so perfect anymore. The kids are not behaving perfectly, the job begins to have problems that feel like trouble, your relationship shifts into low gear, and you see that the perfect person has a few flaws.

Of course you would want to do and have life be perfect, but there are times that your life and they just won't cooperate. You anguish over events that happen to you that make it seem as if what you are doing and how you are is imperfect. Maybe you had a master plan about your life and it turned out in some areas, but you cannot manipulate your plans enough to make it turn out in other areas. Your struggle to discover and manifest perfect makes life look even more imperfect than it might really be.

Choices

There is a lot of press in the world to be perfect and have a perfect life. And everyone has a unique idea of the specifics about perfect. When you accept your life exactly as it is, you have much more control over what perfect means. Perfect seems to be whatever you define it as. What is perfect for you is not perfect for someone else. What is perfect for someone else makes you very uneasy, so you or they condemn the situation as being imperfect. And the irony is that perfect only lives in your definition.

As you live and experience life, you choose to define what things you experience, think, and feel as perfect. You can hold the position that this must be the perfect way for it to be. Things do happen perfectly. The perfect life for you to be living is happening right now.

You can take charge of having a perfect life simply by your definition. Look at the hard issues in your life from a new perspective. Start by declaring that maybe this hard item is not so bad. Create some ease for yourself by the way you think about it. Look closely and intently at the issues to discover the perfection there. It seems so hidden and difficult because it is about you. It's possible that you haven't wanted to look that closely at yourself, but if you look for and concentrate on the perfection of your life, you will discover that life is much less of a struggle. You don't need to know the outcome of specific items or even the outcome of your whole life.

You will find whatever you look for. If you only see imperfection in your life, that is what you will find. If you look for perfection you will also find that. Nothing is not perfect. It all has a purpose, and it all will happen anyway, perfectly. Perfection is only an idea of the mind. Stretch yourself and see perfection, and then you will experience perfection.

> *The nature of imperfect is a detriment;*
> *the nature of perfect is an asset.*

To Do

Be easy on yourself when you are critiquing yourself. Know that you do when you can, and you would if you could. There is nothing wrong with your life except your saying so. When you feel a need to improve items, you do; and when you won't live the way you are anymore, you don't. You have a natural process that perfectly directs you where you want to go. The less you hold yourself and your life as imperfect, the more perfect you become.

Think about whether you can obtain your definition of perfect in one lifetime?

Think perfect of them, and it will be easy to think perfect of yourself.

If you believe that it is not perfect, do what you can do to change it.

When you are trying to be perfect, be like yourself.

Admit to yourself and someone else what you think is perfect about you.

Summarize the many ways that your life is perfect, and share it with someone you admire.

*A
fundamental
misunderstanding
about*

Insight

*is that
you
recognize the
messenger.*

You have been living with yourself for a long time, and it seems as if you should know yourself. However, occasionally you find yourself puzzled by your reactions to another or to certain situations. You can't really discern what's wrong, it's just that you are irritated; you can't seem to explain it, you just know that it is.

There are people who can do nothing to please you. They would do anything to win your favor, but secretly you know you won't like anything they do. Or maybe you've made them wrong because what they do bothers you. If only they would do differently, you wouldn't be so upset—you believe they did it to you; they thought they were just being themselves. Maybe someone else seems pleasant enough but something makes you suspicious. You think they have some hidden agenda with you.

And, there are others you just can't stand. You don't like how they act. They are too self-centered, too stuck-up, or too aloof. They always make you feel uneasy, and you don't want to be around them. You believe they are behaving that way to make you feel unworthy, incapable, or inferior. What about the relatives that you cannot endure one more time? They tell you all your faults, and they always find the exact faults that you are trying to hide.

It may be that others don't bother you but certain situations are your nemesis.

—You believe no one important noticed when you refused to do the job.

—You've repeatedly been fired or had to quit because *they* were at fault.

—You always have trouble getting along with people because they don't understand you.

—You find yourself having trouble with money, and it's sure not your fault.

—People refuse to listen to your ideas and opinions even when you can justify them all.

You may want to carefully consider those times that

others behave in a way that disturbs you or situations arise that you don't like. To understand what is causing the trouble, you may need to look beyond the person or the situation. Those people and situations that have entered your moments may be there to provide you with important insight into yourself.

When people and situations arrive in your life, they have come to be your teacher. If you want your life to expand, you can't spend time blaming people and situations. Therefore, you might ask yourself, what is the real issue here? What are they really doing? What insight can you have?

Choices

It happens that life reflects your internal considerations about yourself. When you hate something about someone or something, think what it tells you about you. Your dis-ease lives inside of you, not outside in them. They are reflecting to you something you think or feel about yourself. You can only fool yourself for so long. Given enough discomfort with enough people or situations, maybe you will look within to see yourself.

—Could it be that you repeatedly get fired because someone with authority threatens your sense of self?

—Could it be that you always see the worst in yourself, so you see that in others?

—Could it be that your image of yourself is connected to how much you have?

—Could it be that you must prove you are generous because you do not feel generous?

—Could it be that you need others' approval because you do not feel credible?

There is very little mystery about life and the message it is giving you. When you look to see what life is reflecting to you about yourself, it will be a full-time job. You will have very little time to wonder whether they are doing something to you.

Each time you learn something about yourself you get more of yourself. When you don't have a need to blame them, you get more of life to live. Space opens for you to live your life with understanding and contentment. You can never get to the end of knowing yourself, so be patient with your teachers. They are giving you valuable insight about you.

> *The nature of knowing-it-all is illusion;*
> *the nature of insight is perception.*

To Do

Blaming or avoiding them prevents you from seeing yourself. But there is no need to worry. If you don't see yourself the first time, it will come up again and again until you do. It is just your *self* trying to communicate something to you about yourself.

Find your role in their attitude toward you before you confront them.

When you confront them, tell them what you did first.

If you are going to tell them your complaints about them, also tell them your complaints about yourself.

When you want to point out their faults, point out yours instead.

Make an agreement with yourself to look for the best in each day.

Dwell on thoughts that make you feel good.

Get busy when thoughts that make you feel bad persist.

A Matter of Choice

A fundamental misunderstanding about

Your Word

is that if you didn't mean it, it doesn't count.

Have you ever wondered why you need to make a promise to get another to believe you? Or is it that others just won't take your words seriously, and sometimes you have to get loud and intense to even get them to hear you? And you may have wondered why it is that your repetition on a point doesn't seem to have any affect on the point at all.

Think about the many times you thought that you were saying something but nothing seemed to get through to them. Your words came out, yet they didn't seem to get the attention you planned. Or when they did get attention, it wasn't the way you hoped.

How many times has missed communication cost you time and created problems? And how many times have you said that you would do something or be someplace and then changed your mind?

—Perhaps you say what you want, when you want, and you don't care what others think because you know that is their problem.

—Perhaps you say what you believe others want to hear and then you do whatever you want.

—Perhaps you say what you need to say to get what you want.

—Perhaps you agree when you need to, never intending to fulfill your agreement.

In small and in large ways, your words can be spoken to confuse, manipulate, control, or sabotage. And all the while you may be believing that it doesn't matter too much because one person won't know what you said to another, they won't catch you, and besides it's not anyone's business.

Your life is going along fine with you putting out the fires that your words have started with family, friends, community, and state. It doesn't seem like much trouble because everyone knows that words don't amount to much. Trouble only happens when you get confused about your words that count and your words that don't count. Sometimes it's hard to keep track, particularly when you want them to believe you and they don't, or you want to believe yourself and you don't, or you can't remember what you committed to, or what story you told to whom.

Actually, communication is a gift and a privilege. You fundamentally live your life alone and your communication, your words, enables you to share an otherwise lonely existence. Your word is too powerful to be given or spoken carelessly. Even if they never catch up with you, your words reflect your inner life. When no one else knows what is true for you, you do. And thoughtless words add up like a pile of rubbish. They collect around you, disguising who you are naturally. They create attitudes of mistrust and deception, and they damage personal and business relationships.

Your words identify your thoughts about yourself and your thoughts about others. They give away your secret considerations about yourself, and they can betray you when you carelessly throw them away.

Your word is what you have to communicate who you are, what you are capable of, and what you want for yourself and others. When you reflect on your life and decide it's time to make changes, notice what you speak; it counts more that you might be aware.

Choices

The value of your word becomes crystal clear when you are communicating about events that tremendously impact your life. These are times that you want to be clearly understood because so much depends upon it. You want another to count on you, understand your position, trust you, or agree with what you say for various reasons.

You realize that it is imperative that they believe your word in order to finalize that big deal. You want them to believe that you are dependable when all that you have to convince them with is your say so. You want them to give you the break you have been waiting for, to believe you can do it.

If you have been in the habit of communicating what you mean and meaning what you communicate, they probably will. However, if you have communicated carelessly and have never troubled to follow through on your word, you may have problems getting them to believe you. The trouble is that you have gotten your point across many ways, many times. You have an aura around you that has been created by your word—an external layer of information that tells others who you really are and what you believe. The closer your relationship to them, the more it tells them. They hear what your words tell them in many ways.

—If you are saying something to patronize them, they sense it.

—If you are telling them something just to have your way in the moment, they realize it.

—If you are committing with no intention, they know it.

The words you choose to communicate, attached to the tone of your communication, delivered by your actions all reveal what you really mean with your word. When you want to make an impact in your own life and in the lives of others, all the components of your communication need to match. Your word is your power to communicate what your intentions are. You won't want to diminish your power by abusing your word.

Use your word to empower yourself and others. They will give back to you the power of your word, and they will reflect to you what you intend. They will appreciate the clarity with which you give your word. They will believe you and trust you.

> *The nature of not honoring your word*
> *is duplicity;*
> *the nature of honoring your word*
> *is respect.*

To Do

The power of your word creates your world. Because in all of the small and large ways you communicate, you are telling things about yourself. Use your word to create a world that is about you. Others will take your word for it when it matches what you intend. They will believe you when *you* believe you. When all of the components of your communication match your word, you will touch them and they will believe you.

When you give your word, plan to do it.

Only give your word freely.

Make it right with all parties concerned if you've gone back on your word.

Think before you commit.

Give your word without hidden motivations.

Agree when you can and keep your agreements.

Give your word in earnest.

Practicing

A fundamental misunderstanding
about practicing
is that
it gets over.

Practicing

All of your life you have received input about who you are, what you should be, and what you need to do to live happily and successfully. You may have had social advantages that others did not that influenced what was important to you. Perhaps you had it all and rejected it, or you had nothing and decided you must get it.

Your spiritual development encouraged you to aspire to live within prescribed guidelines, and your family had their own ideas about your personal development and how you should turn out. Very early your behavior was encouraged or discouraged, depending upon your family's values. Maybe you developed your own principles, inspired by your peers or personal interests.

However it happened, while you were growing, you were deciding about who you are and what is important to you. You began to collect the content that you call yourself. And you began to identify with it.

—Perhaps you think you are the amount of money you have. If you have a lot, you think you are worth a lot; if you have a little, you think you are worth a little.

—Perhaps you think you are your job. If your job is successful, you think that you are successful; if your job is not, you think you are not.

—Perhaps you think you are your relationships. When your relationships are good, you think that you are good, lovable, stable, secure, or successful. When your relationships are not so good, you think that you are unlovable, unstable, insecure, and unsuccessful.

—Perhaps you have come to identify yourself as someone who doesn't have to, because your position is influence enough. Or you may think that you can't, because you have no influence in your position.

—Perhaps you identify yourself as physically able or lazy and then you credit or discredit the content of your life, depending on your physical capabilities. You would do what you love to do; however, you are always too sick, too tired, too fat, too thin, too short, too tall, or too unable.

Living itself brings this content into your life. All of your guarding, avoiding, conniving, denying, and downright lying won't eliminate content. Content is the stuff of life—the dramas, the attachments, the encounters that you have each day you are living. The content is not your life. You don't have to identify with it; you do have choices about it. When you decide that you want to, you can begin to think differently about how you live your life. Then you will know that what you make of the content is what determines your experience of living.

Naturally, making new decisions and choices has challenges. It might seem difficult to change your mind, your job, your relationships, or your environment. But choosing lightness brings changes that you already know are needed. Without change you are stuck and in a rut. And besides, the pain, despair, or boredom of your content will move you on toward living your life in a manner that demonstrates your desire to be a lighter you.

*A
fundamental
misunderstanding
about*

Content

*is that
you know
what will
happen.*

As you think about your life you feel resentful or grateful, successful or not, confused or clear about your past and present content. You find yourself living content that you did not initiate, that you don't deserve, and that you don't want.

You have spent time and money trying to work out and work through present and past content that you do not like. Sometimes you don't bother to work on it—you simply pretend that it does not belong to your life.

However, content has a way of influencing every aspect of your life. Some content you consider your ally, other content you consider your enemy. Some content wakes you up to the realization that you are living, some answers your need for integration, and some aligns you with your dreams.

Because content makes such an impact, there is a tendency to try and manipulate it. You swear by it, you make deals to avoid it, and you make plans so it will never happen. You have mental lists of just what you will deal with and just what you won't, often to no avail. You decide, for example,

—they can't talk to you like that, and they do.

—that can't be happening to you, and it is.

—your kids would never do that, and they did.

—you would never work there, and you do.

—they would never divorce you, and they did.

—you would never go there, and you went.

—you can't live without X, and you are.

—you will never have that, and you do.

No matter your best thought-out plans, everything can and will happen to you. What you plan for will happen, and what you don't plan for will happen. What you want will happen, and what you don't want will happen. What you like and what you don't like will also happen. And, of course, they will do what you never thought they would do, and you will deal with things you never thought you would.

Knowing that everything can and does happen gives you space to lighten up. The question is not how to avoid it happening, but what to do about it once it happens. Some things you have choices about what to *do* about them, others you have choices about how to *be* about them. But you do have choices about the way you live your content.

Choices

You are the one that gives the power of devastation or joy to your content. You have the choice because you are the master of your content. You only feel victimized by your life's content when you give in to believing that you are your content. When you think that you are your relationship, your job, your possessions, or your status, you begin to believe and act on those beliefs in a manner that keeps you trapped in the very content you hate. All the sorrow, guilt, blame, and insecurity that you feel for yourself and others will produce more of the same until you admit that this is for you to do something about or to see in a new way.

You cannot master your content while believing that you are your content. Mastery happens the instant you realize that you choose. You choose to live without attachment to your content because you are not your job, your money, your relationship, your status, or your problems.

When you discover what really matters to you, the drama of your content won't be so heavy because you will know how to choose. You won't have a need to escape the present or past. You will embrace what has happened and what is happening simply because it is your life that is happening.

While you are living your content, you are constantly making decisions about your life. Some parts of your life you cherish and other parts you despise. Content has been your motivation to make changes, to forgive, to love, and to think about the life you are living. So embrace all of your life and own it as yours. The content that you like and the content that you don't like belongs to you.

You cannot be your own master, you cannot be at choice until you are ready to take charge. When you are ready, you will choose to forgive and forget, persevere rather than quit, have compassion for yourself and others, love unconditionally, give thanks for what you have, and be mindful that you have the option to be the master of your content. When you do, it will change.

> *The nature of disowning content is avoidance; the nature of mastering content is acceptance.*

To Do

Underneath your content you are a whole person. You already have all of the qualities that you need to live fully and completely. When you access your wholeness, you have the answers to your questions, the solutions to your problems, and the ability to fulfill your desires.

Choose your way to deal with your content.

Choose to forgive their betrayal even though you are advised not to.

Love rather than begrudge your childhood.

Apply for the job that will be a challenge.

Choose to initiate friendships.

Be nice to them when they think you will be angry.

Choose what is appropriate to you.

Take care of your physical content.

Review the significance of your financial content.

Choose not to be abused.

Choose what it is about it that holds meaning for you.

A fundamental misunderstanding about

Caring

is that they determine how you care.

Sometimes others think you care too much. They warn you of doom and gloom if you let your caring get you too involved. And, if you ask, everyone has a different opinion about what "too involved" means. They have opinions about how interested you are, the amount of help you lend, the amount of support you give, and other actions that say to another that you are on their side.

Their concern may be genuine because caring can be demanding and emotionally debilitating. You care about others for various reasons, and you are willing to interact with their lives to let them know that you care. But if your caring becomes a struggle for you, it is time to reevaluate your endeavors. It is time to ask yourself why you care so much.

—Do you care because you have expectations? You want something special from them so you do a few things to let them know you care.

—Do you care because you are in a relationship and you have learned there are things you must do or they won't think you care?

—Do you care because you don't know what else you would do if you didn't have them to care about?

—Do you care because they provide for you and you don't believe you could provide for yourself?

—Do you care so much because this may be the only person who likes you?

—Do you care so much because they are the only one who makes you feel good about yourself?

The trouble with caring from hidden motives is that you expect something from them for your caring, and they expect something in return for letting you care.

Choices

Genuine caring has no expectations; it has the element of freedom. A gift of caring lets go of the gift; whatever you have given or give is free—it has no charge. You don't expect them to do something in return for the favor. You don't expect them to behave a particular way. They will behave many ways because life requires them to live many events, and you will care for them through it all.

You don't expect that you will get a reward. The reward is that your caring for them results in your caring for yourself. You don't expect that they will be there forever just because you care for them. This is not an issue when you are caring moment to moment.

Caring is a natural outcome of loving who you are. When you feel wonderful about yourself, what you naturally do is care about others and you naturally know what to do to provide evidence of your caring. Caring happens on the inside of you and then you produce evidence on the outside. You want to give them the attention of your caring. You want them to know that you and they are important.

If they have come to expect fixed responses from you, they have become oblivious to the gift you have given them with your caring. Caring is a special gift and you don't want it to be abused. Caring speaks about your inner self; you will want to respect this and be selective, because genuine caring helps you interpret the truth about yourself and those you care about. If you care for them freely with no expectations, others will consider it a privilege to be a part of your life. They will approach you for the purity of your caring because it heals and enhances their life.

> *The nature of manipulative caring is abuse;
> the nature of genuine caring is love.*

To Do

You cannot care too much. If there is a problem, it is because you cannot care about yourself enough to extend that gift to others. Care all you want. Produce evidence of your caring all you want. When you genuinely care, you are on their side, and they are on your side. The quality with which you care will be reflected in the quality with which you are cared about. You will know if you have cared freely because they will return your caring.

Choose not to manipulate and call it "caring."

Care about your time before you get involved.

If it feels like a sacrifice, reconsider.

Care that they want to make it right with you.

Care first what it means to you before you consider what it means to them.

Care about them when you are mad.

Care that they are doing the best they can.

*A
fundamental
misunderstanding
about*

Sharing

*is that
they are
supposed
to.*

There are no rules about sharing except the ones that you have made for yourself or the ones that you agree to. What you share and how you share are major considerations when you are in relationship. Time together will teach you what you want to share as it will teach them what they want to share with you.

Your experience of sharing will clearly demonstrate to you what your motivations for sharing are about.

—Perhaps you share to win approval. You don't share what they don't like.

—Perhaps you share as a means of controlling. You shouldn't do X, Y, or Z so you don't share that you are doing it.

—Perhaps you share only what you have to. In the past you shared everything, and it got you into trouble so you just quit telling them about yourself.

—Perhaps you share to make them responsible. You won't share unless they start, because why should they know something about you that you don't know about them.

—Perhaps you share to get something they wouldn't want to give. You think if you can say the right thing, true or not, they will give it to you.

—Perhaps you share to make yourself look good or to make them look bad. You don't feel equal, and you need to be one-up.

—Perhaps you can't share too much because you haven't been honest. If they knew what you were really up to, they might leave you.

—Perhaps you don't share much at all anymore because they are always critical.

If you find yourself censoring, you have become a critic not a partner. Choosing not to share will limit the boundaries of your relationship. You cannot assume that they will share what you are not willing to share. Sharing with the motivation of cricitism may satisfy you in the short term but it will adversely affect your intimate relationship.

Choices

You cannot be on the inside of someone else's experience. Fortunately, you can create a safe environment with them, one that lets them know you are interested in their life. When that happens, you will want to share with them and they will want to share with you.

Safety, not agreement, creates intimate sharing. You may have already discovered that none of your agreements can control the affairs of another's heart. You realize that some of their issues have very little to do with you. If they feel safe to share their issues, you will be like a best friend. So be wise, and spend your extra time controlling your own issues. You won't have anything to hide, and you will feel free to share. It is useless to try controlling another's issues; they will do what they must do.

Consider it a privilege if they share the affairs of their heart with you, for it means that you have created a safe environment through your approval. They are in the mood to let you in on their secrets. They find comfort in your acknowledgment that their life is about them, and they will be inclined to share it with you.

You will get to share their life while they are coming along, growing older, growing different, and growing wiser. You will not miss out when you are available to share the affairs of the heart with each other.

> The nature of secrecy causes suspicion;
> the nature of sharing expands your relationship.

To Do

When you are in relationship with someone, you will have the opportunity to share many events. You will share your sadness and your joy and everything in between. It is wonderful to have another that shares your concerns, your plans, your present, and your future. You will want to do things to maintain what you share, and you will want to do things to further what you share.

Share as much good news as bad news.

Be attentive when they share with you.

Share to acknowledge.

Share to express affection.

Share to express commitment.

Share to comfort.

Share to learn.

Share to create a life together.

*A
fundamental
misunderstanding
about*

Arguing

*is that
you can
win
something.*

When you are in relationship with someone who has an opinion about everything you do, everything you think, and every way you are, it takes a lot of energy to communicate with them. They tend to argue with you about items that are not relevant to anything. There are times it seems as if they argue with you for some reason only they know about.

—They argue to get attention. It's likely that they have learned some attention is better than none and an argument gets your attention.

—They argue because they already had the conversation with you in their mind.

—They argue because they need to feel important. They believe you will see how important they are if they can win the argument.

—They argue because they have underlying issues with you. Maybe they have previous agendas with you that have not been settled and arguing with you is their way of letting you know something is not OK.

—They argue because they are competitive with you.

—They argue because they have no other recourse with you. They believe you are unapproachable about particular situations.

—They argue because they want you to know that they have a fine mind. Maybe they do not feel credible with you.

—They argue because they misunderstood your position. There are times that you discover you both hold the same position, said different ways.

—They argue out of habit. Arguing is a way of life for them. They believe they win something.

Choices

Arguing expends energy and limits your desire and ability to communicate. Sometimes you get discouraged before you even begin communicating with them. You realize they already have their mind made up, and you can't think of anything you can tell them that won't begin an argument. The problem with arguing is that no one wins. Notice who feels good about it and what they got. Someone will come away from the argument feeling unsatisfied.

When they feel they must argue their point, they have more invested in their opinions than seems evident. They have a need to win something that they do not possess inside of themselves. Their need to win the argument tells you that they do not naturally feel good about their position; if they can win the argument, it justifies that position.

There is an easy solution about arguing. Let them have their position without arguing with them. What does it cost you? You can believe what you believe and do what you do without needing to win an argument. You can agree that they have a point even though you know inside that it is not applicable to you. You already know you can enjoy conversations with others that don't end up in dead ends or losses. Arguing your way through life is a struggle, and giving up the struggle costs nothing.

When you are confident on the inside, you don't have to win because you already have. You know what is so for you, and you don't have to prove it by arguing with them. The best way to end an argument is by letting them be right. The argument is finished when someone is right. And you will have more energy because you haven't dissipated it by arguing.

A Matter of Choice

> *The nature of arguing is discord;*
> *the nature of agreeing is harmony.*

To Do

If arguing is a common way to pass time, maybe you can look at why you need to be passing time. When your life is full and you are doing what you need and want to do, it leaves little time for arguing. Rarely can you get them to do what they don't want to do or feel someway they don't want to feel by arguing with them.

Suggest new solutions to familiar arguments.

Find one new thing that you are interested in together.

Listen to their whole point before you begin yours.

Discuss critical issues after mad is over.

Check to see if you are arguing over the same point of view.

Enroll them in your life, and be enrolled in theirs.

*A
fundamental
misunderstanding
about*

Forgiveness

*is that
you can
forgive
and remember.*

When relationships are long term, many things happen in them. They have a lot of history behind them. Sometimes you are happy and content, other times they make you frustrated and angry. Some agendas in relationship are small and insignificant; others are large and shattering. Maybe they embarrassed you, and you are not about to forget it. Maybe they have had an affair, and you feel betrayed. Maybe they did *the* thing that is the final straw for you.

Whatever, you are determined to hide your anger, but you know you are going to get them. You want them to get the point, one way or another, that they are in disfavor with you. Maybe you let it pass momentarily, and pretend that everything is all right. But secretly you know you are waiting to get them. You wait for the right opportunity to pull a bullet out of your pocket to shoot them with when they are the most vulnerable. You do it because you did not forgive them, and you did not forget. Maybe you have lots of ammunition.

There are bullets aimed at self-esteem.

—*Yes, you did this OK, but remember when you did that other terrible thing.*

—*Can't you manage anything I tell you to do?*

—*I told you so.*

There are bullets aimed at control.

—*Can I count on you this time?*

—*You aren't going to try that again are you? Remember when you failed before?*

—*I expected you would foul up; you always do.*

There are bullets to make you look better than they look.

—*I always do, and you never do.*

—*You never give, and I always give.*

—*You are always against me, and I shouldn't expect it to be any different this time.*

There are bullets to defend yourself.

—You do that so I might as well do this.

—You don't care about me so why should I care about you?

—I've tried everything while you have done nothing.

—I did for you but you never did for me.

You can justify your need to collect bullets about all of their shortcomings, mistakes, favors, and sacrifices. You are saving bullets to give you some recourse against insult, hurt, anger, frustration, not getting your way, making your point, or other self interests. When you collect bullets, you have ammunition for the next time they hurt you. You have an arsenal to remind them that you are right and they are wrong. Sometimes you shoot a bullet with such deadly aim that they are injured forever.

Choices

It's difficult to be in relationship and let the past be the past. The natural tendency is to let the past add up to particular conclusions about your relationship. Part of you wants them to know you, and you want to know them. But knowing and being known makes you vulnerable. Some things hurt you, frustrate you, anger you. When you can really forgive them, you get to have a special relationship where you and they can live life fully, knowing you are on their side and they are on your side.

—It keeps your relationship with them fresh and clean. You are not using your encounters with them to collect bullets or to be defensive. Each encounter is new and safe.

—You will feel free and unburdened. Saving and collecting bullets to get them is dangerous—they can explode in your own pocket. Besides, you cause them to start saving bullets also. The wars of your relationship are made up from the bullets in your pockets. You may win a few battles, but you will still be at war.

—Your life in relationship can be about something more than them keeping you in line or you keeping them in line.

When you can forgive them, you can also forgive yourself for being human. When you can forgive them, you don't have to hide from each other. Living together is hard enough; having to hide yourself makes it almost impossible to be glad you are in relationship.

You want to forgive them because bullets hurt. You get injured, and so do they. If there are too many bullets, they eventually kill your relationship. Forgiving them is as much about you as it is about them. When you forgive them, you start over. You have a new beginning. You forget it. You appreciate where they are vulnerable, and you never use it to get them. You understand that in the course of living a lifetime with someone you love, you and they will need to be forgiven and to have it forgotten.

> *The nature of bullets is spite;*
> *the nature of forgiveness is compassion.*

To Do

Forgiving means it's over. It's over and all of the stuff about it is over. Search for any remnants of the event, and drop them. It literally means forgetting that it happened. It gives you a new start with a clean slate, and no bullets to carry around with you.

Want to forgive them.

Tell them they are forgiven.

Drop it so completely that you know you will never bring it up again.

Forgive something from your past.

Forgive them for being inconsiderate.

Forgive yourself for the time you think you let yourself down.

Forgive them for not forgetting.

Forgive the same issue more than once.

*A
fundamental
misunderstanding
about*

Love

*is that
they have
something
to do with it.*

People think differently about love, and they have different requirements about love. Some think the one they love only returns that love when particular behavior is expressed. Others think that they have to produce certain evidence or the one they love will not believe they share love together. Still others believe that they don't have to do anything, and their love will just maintain itself. There are those who know the love they share is changing, yet they are determined to keep it confined. Still others believe they can manipulate love to force it in the direction they want.

Maybe you promised and they promised that your love would endure. Maybe your promise was to your children, and you have given them the best of everything and now they want little to do with you. Or was it to a significant other who has become a stranger to you? Was it to a special person that has told you goodbye? And when you notice that it is on its way to over, what do you do?

—Some people hope to influence love by making more demands. They feel the energy of love weakening so they demand more attention, more answers, more plans, more of everything that love can no longer provide.

—Others hope to influence love by becoming something that the loved one wants or needs them to be. Insidiously, their loving masks the sacrifices being made until the demands on their self cost them more than they can give.

—Others hope to buy love, denying or providing according to the mood love finds itself in. They turn love on when all is well and turn love off when it is not.

Unfortunately, love can and does fade like a shadow. It gives cause for great frustration when you have invested your life and your energy in this loved one, and it begins to vanish right before your eyes. You wonder what has gone wrong, what did you do, where did the magic of your love go? You begin to question what you have thought about love.

—Do you believe they no longer love you because they are acting different? Within what boundaries should they be acting for you to be assured that they love you?

—Do you believe they no longer love you because they have developed their own ideas about their life? Are they wanting to be more self-expressive, and you find it threatening?

—Do you believe they no longer love you because they no longer share everything with you? Are they withdrawing from you because something is wrong, or is life full at this time and they have other things on their mind?

—Do you believe they no longer love you because you have changed? Have you been afraid to follow some of your dreams for fear they won't love or support you anymore?

—Do you believe they no longer love you because they would never have treated you this way before? Are they treating you this way because of you or because of them?

—Do you believe they no longer love you because they have a new focus in their life? Can you share love even when you have other major focuses?

So much of the time you get used to the way your love looks and feels. You hadn't planned for it to look and feel different ways. And when it does look and feel differently, it surprises you and you begin to make assumptions and draw conclusions about your love based on the information you have been in the mood to collect.

Loving and being loved is a great paradox that you won't want to miss in life. Actually it requires less from you, not more. Often it wants you to let it be whatever or wherever it is. It wants to teach you what you need to know. If you are looking, you will discover that there may be ways to think about love other than the ways you previously made up.

Choices

Love belongs to you. It is yours to uniquely express as you please. You can acknowledge it or not, you can express it or not, you can share it or not. But whatever you choose, your loving is a responsibility that belongs only to you.

Love looks like it belongs to the one you love. It looks as if they determine the outcome of your loving them. However, love is personally yours, and they can only influence your love if you choose. Their behavior, manipulation, withdrawal, or sacrifice cannot influence something that is not theirs.

It may seem that you must stop loving because they have stopped loving. However, loving is a feeling that makes *you* feel good. It makes no difference where they are in reference to where your love is. Your love lives where you live; therefore you can experience it at any time you want and under any set of circumstances.

Loving is easier than not loving. It happens that when you just let love and be love, it will express itself perfectly to achieve the results that you want. It is very difficult to stop loving them when the love lives inside of you. In fact, love helps you feel the inside of yourself. Is it an accident that hearts are a universal symbol for love? Your heart actually feels full of your love and the energy of it overflows, washing over those coming in contact with the fullness of your love.

Love is a becoming. You are love becoming itself; love is you becoming yourself. Love is most familiar to you because it is you. There are no troubles or differences in the space of love. When love is full, every item on your list of issues is fine.

> *The nature of forcing love is pretense;*
> *the nature of letting love is authentic.*

To Do

Loving is so personally yours that you can finally celebrate. It is a gift given to you to let you know your worth. When love is not abused by rejection or demands, it lives inside of you as a symbol that you are free; choosing and living unconditionally.

Love them no matter where they are.

A Matter of Choice

Be easy on yourself.

Do a small service for the very one you are upset with.

Do a large service for the one that needs it most.

Make a phone call to spread good will.

Acknowledge, apologize, amend.

Do a good deed that begins with each letter of the alphabet.

*A
fundamental
misunderstanding
about*

Problems

> *is that
> what looks
> like one
> is one.*

If you knew that this was the last evening you were ever to spend with the person you love, how would you want to spend your time? Would you spend it going over all of your problems, or would those problems seem trivial to you? Suddenly, everything you thought was a problem may seem minor in contrast. You would want to make every moment with your person count and tell them everything that you needed to tell them before your time was up.

How casually do you spend your time with the one you love? Do you tend to expect that they will be there for all of your tomorrows so you can afford to throw away your time in relationship with them? Sometimes you forget that all of your moments with them count, and any one of them could be your last one with them. Do you want the last moment to be one of grudges and irritations?

When you are in relationship, you have the inclination to troubleshoot and look for impending problems. You want to get them settled before they get out of control. You spend your time together in deep discussion about today's problems, yesterday's problems, and tomorrow's problems.

—It may be that you look for problems to haggle over because that is what you are used to doing in relationship.

—It may be that you just don't care enough about your relationship to consider if what you think and do will create a problem.

—It may be that you believe it's their problem, and it doesn't affect you.

—It may be that you feel relieved that you have someone to share all of your problems with.

—It may be that you would rather have problems with them than spend your energy looking for solutions.

—It may be that you want to test them to see how many problems you can have, and still have a relationship.

—It may be that you have no relationship except your

problems, their problems, and the problems you have together.

Maybe you can see just how fragile life is, and still you continue to indulge in behavior that does not add dimension to your life or your relationship. Maybe you believe that if you can just get through today, you can start tomorrow letting them know how much you appreciate being in relationship with them. Maybe you believe that if you can just get the next six problems solved, then you would enjoy being in relationship.

When you assume your relationship is a great place to create and solve all of your problems, your dream-come-true relationship can turn into a nightmare saturated with nothing but problems. You might want to consider that when you look for problems or believe that if there are problems, they must be worth the risk. Your relationship is being built around those items that are most important to you, ones that you want in your relationship, ones that are about your relationship. When you are not careful and you casually introduce problems into your relationship, your relationship becomes about problems. You might discover that you are missing many good times because you have indulged in problems. In fact, you have blown them out of proportion because you have dwelt on them so much.

Choices

Sometimes you make up problems before they arrive, and sometimes you ignore problems that have already arrived. Either way you have more problems than you started with.

It might be an interesting experiment to become very clear about problems. Consider them and choose if you want to add them to your relationship. The idea is to decide when a problem is truly a problem. Is it important to bring it up, to hash it over, process it, or talk about it yet one more time?

Find other avenues to express yourself within your relationship. What your person really wants most is the best of you. Perhaps you could consider it a challenge. Problems are only problems by your declaration. And relationships have many challenges. You will spend enough energy finding solutions to your genuine challenges. Life with someone you love and care about will seem too short anyway.

The nature of problems in relationship is conflict;
the nature of solutions in relationship is peace.

To Do

An interesting phenomena about relationships is that, over the course of a lifetime, everything will happen. Sometimes they will be wonderful, sometimes they will be busy, sometimes they will be sad, other times they will be strange. If you decide that all of these happenings are problems, you will miss the challenge of them. When you have problems, you are looking for sympathy. When you have a challenge, you are looking for solutions.

Discuss with your person what issues you can classify as challenges rather than problems.

Make an agreement together that your relationship works.

Pick one item that you can forget as a problem.

Accept that they are different from you, and that they do different than you.

Tell them you don't want your relationship to be about problems, and decide what you do want it to be about.

Have good will toward them.

Find a way to be for them, not against them.

A fundamental misunderstanding about

Falling In Love

*is that
it is
always
what you think.*

Falling in love has been blamed for thousands of scenarios with serious consequences. If your feelings have gotten the best of you and your better judgment is dramatically altered, you may be mistaken about the issue of love. Maybe even you are suspicious of yourself, because overnight you changed from easygoing to someone who can't keep it together.

—It could be that the person you have met is the object of your secret fantasies.

—It could be your hormones are running rampant.

—It could be that you believe you are their rescuer.

—It could be that you are needy.

—You could have mistaken sex for love.

—You could be fascinated with their undivided attention.

—You could be using it as an excuse to break some other promise.

—They could be manipulating you to get some favor.

—They could be desperate to have someone to possess.

—They could be satisfying your lack of confidence.

There is a difference between falling in love and becoming obsessed. Obsession involves ulterior motives that promise few gains and many losses. Obsession intensely demands, with little regard for your integrity. Often you find yourself behaving bizarrely, becoming a stranger to yourself and others.

Choices

If you are faced with decisions about love yet one more time, you will want to know if it is love you are feeling or a temporary obsession.

—Lasting love comes without conditions. You don't have any, and neither do they. You and they have many conditions when it is obsession.

—Lasting love is not a secret—you want everyone to know. On the other hand, obsession often has many secrets, and you want few people to know.

—Lasting love enhances, and does nothing to detract. Obsession consumes your life, leaving trouble in its wake.

—Lasting love is expansive, and you want to share them with your friends. Obsession wants them reserved all for you.

—Lasting love has commitments for a future together. Obsession often doesn't want to consider it.

—Lasting love has the patience to endure problems. Obsession usually doesn't want to talk about troubles; they ruin the fun.

— Lasting love will require that you give and take. Obsession can be a one-way street.

When you find yourself struggling with the issue, ask yourself, "Is this love or obsession, and what are the consequences?" If you understand what love has to offer over obsession, you would wait until you have the courage to find love. Love manifests when you are ready, and it carries a message with it—one that is very personal to you. You will know if it is love or obsession because you will get the point.

> *The nature of obsession is temporary;*
> *the nature of love is permanence.*

To Do

Obsession called love has many guises, but if lasting love has found you, you will surely know it. They will be the perfect person no matter what sex, race, or religion. It won't matter what others' opinions are. You and your person will make a perfect match. You will have little trouble smoothing out the ripples that your togetherness creates.

Take your time; if it is love, it will be there later.

Fix the relationship you have, and see if obsession remains.

Tell those you care for about it.

Notice what it adds to your life.

Notice if it threatens your life.

Visualize your life with them.

Make only those promises that you can fulfill.

Be celibate for three months.

*A
fundamental
misunderstanding
about*

Sex

*is that
it is
about
you.*

Minds have every conceivable notion about sex.

—There is good sex, which is proper and requires little adventure.

—There is shy sex that inhibits closeness.

—There is poor sex that is only concerned with reaching orgasm.

—There is private sex that never reveals each other to the partner.

—There is intense sex that satisfies energy release.

—There is angry sex that believes you owe it to them, or they owe it to you.

—There is symptom sex used to cure what ails the relationship.

—There are one-night stands that have no meaning.

—There are long-term affairs that feed the ego.

You may want to consider the various reasons you have sex with another. Sex is often used as a means to evaluate, control, manipulate, or demand.

Many times sex is such a sensitive issue that you avoid revealing yourself much at all. You participate, secretly pretending in your mind that you are with someone else, or are someplace else, or are doing something else. You may want to ask yourself why you are in a sexual situation if you do not want to know your sexual partner or you do not want them to know you.

—Maybe you are only interested in physical release.

—Perhaps you are using sex to repair damage done in an unpleasant encounter.

—Maybe you use sex to remind yourself that you are desirable.

—Or there are times that you consent to have sex with someone to get something you want from them.

No one, at any time, for any reason, owes you sex. You aren't obligated, and neither are they. Used with ulterior motives, sex gives you temporary relief from your issue.

One of the reasons for having sex is that you want to feel good, and it is one way that you achieve this desire. But many other benefits await you when you deeply examine what's available from sharing the privilege of sex. It is the most intimate expression of love that you have been invited to share.

Choices

The closeness experienced in sex often communicates those feelings that words seem unable to express. Suddenly, in those moments, you know and they know what you feel about yourself and about them.

Consider what you want your sexual encounters to say to another, and with this idea in mind you can begin to make decisions about the quality of your sexual life. To express your love for another you might want to find out what would make a wonderful sexual experience for them.

It is possible to create sex as an experience of discovery together. They allow you to witness their discovery of their own pleasure. You become privy to their encounter with themselves. You become the recipient of the energy of their sexual expression. You derive great pleasure in letting the progression of their experience be your guide.

You never forget that they are allowing you to enter into the secret domain of their most vulnerable self. You remember that your sexual participation with them is a privilege. Your countenance will tell them that you cherish this intimate moment of sharing with them.

You can choose to have sex because you want the one you love to know just how much you love them. You can take the opportunity to share sex with them as an expression of your love.

You tenderly and thoughtfully create a space for them to feel open and free with you. You want them to reach beyond the fantasy of their minds and get present to you and to themselves. You want them to know your desire is for them to have pleasure for themselves, and that their pleasure gives you pleasure.

To create pleasure for them requires that you are with them in a way that they can reveal their sexual pleasure to you and most of all to themselves. To experience intimate sex, create it to be about them. It is their body, their mind, their soul that you encounter when you have sex with them. Then you get to be the recipient of the sexual energy that they generate.

The more sex is about them, the deeper they can touch

inside of themselves. They will be free to allow the longing to experience themselves emerge. You will be able to create sex a brand new experience with them each time.

> *The nature of submissive sex is passive;*
> *the nature of consenting sex is privilege.*

To Do

The energy expressed in sex is either negative or positive. Negative energy creates ill will toward yourself and others. The positive expression of sexual energy creates the feeling of intimate connection with another. The feelings you experience with your sexual partner have far-reaching implications. Ultimately, the quality you create about sex will come back to you in other facets of your life.

Have sex with them because you want to.

Learn one new intimate thing about them the next time you have sex.

Let them know you care about them before you want sex with them.

Consider what sex with them means to you, and tell them.

Settle the disagreement before you have sex.

Choose not to use sex to control or manipulate.

Start early when you want to have sex later.

*A
fundamental
misunderstanding
about*

Jealousy

*is that
they
make you
jealous.*

Jealousy is one of those emotions that does not discriminate. At times it arrives without much warning, like the time your other spoke to an old flame more personally than you thought appropriate. Other times you know it is coming, like the time you could no longer believe the same voice got the wrong number twenty-five times.

This mighty antagonist stresses the most solid relationship, whether you are on the offensive or the defensive side of jealousy. When you are on the offensive side of jealousy, like the time you were elusive just to arouse their suspicion, your desire is to get an edge. You might feel you need an edge because

— you want to be reassured of their interest in you;

—you want more attention than you are receiving;

—you want to get something from them that they don't want to give you;

—you think that an edge will insure the position that you want.

Besides you know them, and their vulnerabilities and their jealousy has sometimes benefited you one way or another. You've lived the same scenario many times. After the quarrel of accusation and denial, you got their attention, you got their promise, you got their renewed interest, and you got what you think you still want. And after the all-night conversation and confessions, mutually you agree that trust is an important element in good relationships. In good faith, they decide that there isn't any real cause for them to be jealous, and you are forgiven and even appreciated. Making up has stimulated your relationship, and now that they understand that they are not the only fish in the pond, you can get back to your regular relationship.

Or you may be on the defensive side of jealously. They have, once again, concocted a story that not even their mother would believe. They actually thought you would believe that nothing happened when they met their "ex" for dinner.

Now you are at the end of your patience, and you intend to be smarter this time around. You plan to confront them and demand that they behave within the limits of your tolerance. You are determined to put an end to your jealousy, and you plan to get your point across because you have all the evidence you need. All your friends agree that you are being taken for a fool, and you cannot be expected to live like this.

You may have thought there is a big difference between the sides of jealously you are on. Ultimately, there isn't. On close examination, there is a subtle quality about jealously that makes it unique—if you are making someone jealous you feel justified, and if you are jealous you feel justified. On either side, there is no way you feel good about yourself.

Jealousy fed will grow bigger, whether you are the offender or the offended. It always makes you suffer with the anxiety of wanting what you don't have.

However, if you understand the uniqueness of jealousy, you might be able to make choices that defuse the game before it gets out of hand. One day you might determine that they can't make you jealous or that you won't be jealous because you don't want it anymore. You chose the relationship, the job, or the friends that you have for good reasons. You won't want to let jealousy force you to quit with these people before you look closely at this issue.

Choices

Jealousy take two, and it is a no-win game to play. No one is innocent in the game of jealousy. Honestly look at your situation to determine your role. Ask yourself what you get, wanted or not, from jealousy being a part of your life. The nature of jealousy is that it is interactive, while other emotions are not necessarily. You may not be in relationship with anyone, and still you can experience fear, worry, depression, anger, or a variety of other emotions. But you don't sit at home void of relationship and experience jealousy. Jealousy is a two-party issue.

If you are jealous of them, what are you thinking about yourself? Believe in yourself enough so that you know if they betray you, it is their loss. Always think of yourself as worthy, and you will be. Don't try to change them; if you need a change, change you. They will respond to your desire to have a relationship that is freeing.

Together you can create, in your relationship, space free of jealousy. Just keep your connection with them open, whether you are in their presence or not. And trust yourself to live in a manner that includes them rather than excludes them. Assure them that you are not out to do harm by your actions towards them.

What will make jealousy go away is to work together to be a team—to be on each other's side. When you are for someone they know it; and when they are for you, you know it. And jealousy disappears without a word.

> *The nature of jealousy is low esteem;*
> *the nature of trust is high esteem.*

To Do

When you find yourself jealous of someone, what do you need to do about the way you are in relationship? When you find someone being jealous of you, what do you need to do about the way you are in relationship?

Include them when you notice that they are wanting something from you.

Find ways to assure yourself that you are an asset in relationship.

Take time to talk it over and find a mutual ground about the issue.

Acknowledge them when the opportunity arises.

Understand that their living their life may have parts that are not about you.

Make a rule that you don't want to do jealousy.

A fundamental misunderstanding about

Divorce

is that when it's over, it's over.

"For better or for worse, for richer or for poorer, in sickness and in health, till death do us part" are familiar and powerful vows that people make with each other. When you decided to bond with another, you knew that you would be living your lives together. And when you made those vows, you meant them—you were convinced of your mutual promises. However, as the days and years passed, you may have begun to question the promises you made.

—You didn't think that you would grow apart, and now you have.

—You didn't think that they would be abusive.

—You didn't think that you would meet X and fall in love.

—You didn't think that they would meet Y and fall in love.

—You didn't think that you would ever feel anything but love for them, and now they seem like a total stranger.

—You didn't think that they would be so demanding, jealous, boring, or difficult.

—You don't know how it happened, but you just don't want to live with them anymore.

—You don't know how it happened, but they just don't want to live with you anymore.

When you find yourself considering separation and divorce, you will discover that all of your friends and relatives have opinions about it, especially that you should or you shouldn't or that you are justified or not. You may seek professional counseling in an effort to find answers to the problems that plague the relationship. You may read books about communication and fair fighting. You may try many different things to fix the relationship, such as going to a separation and divorce group and finding out how other people do it. Ultimately you may seek the advice of a divorce lawyer.

How do you determine whether or not you are going to get a divorce? You may find yourself for days and years on the see-saw of "It's a go, it's a no-go," living one day on-again, one day quit-again.

People decide to stay married for all kinds of reasons—finances, family and social pressure, the children, wanting to avoid the massive changes that it will mean, fear of the unknown. If you have been married for ten years, and spent eight of those years wondering if you should unmarry, you may realize that you are not going to get that divorce, for whatever reason. Then free yourself from the vice of indecision by deciding to be where you are. You are married: you are living with them. Give up the mind games that you play, and put your energy into creating the relationship as you want it to be.

Choose to live your life married; choose to stop blaming your life on the marriage. You know how that sounds. "If only I weren't married to X, I would do Y." Well, do Y anyway. If you begin to get the life that you want, the decision about divorce will come clearer. You are not divorced until you are divorced. Living in the limbo of indecision paralyzes you. If you are living with them, live with them until you don't.

Perhaps you feel forced into divorce because your other did the one thing that you can't live with. However, you may discover that you still love them and still want to live with them, but wonder how you can ever forgive and forget it.

And sometimes divorce arrives like a bolt from the sky, and you are stricken down with its intensity and finality. You didn't expect it, and now they want out.

From whichever side it comes, in whatever guise, finally, you know that it is over. You may have come and gone so many times from the marriage that finally you are driven to the decision.

Choices

No one person can fulfill all of your dreams, desires, wishes, and needs. Nor can you fulfill all of theirs. And if you are living your whole life with someone else, it will look many ways. They change; you change. Adjustments are made. Some years are better than others.

But if the marriage is over, it is over. You know. You recognize that the relationship is complete. You are no longer angry; they don't push all of your buttons; you don't spend your time thinking up ways to get even with them. It is just done.

When it is complete, you will be less likely to repeat the same relationship again. Often if people divorce to get rid of a problem, they find that same problem in a different disguise in their next relationship.

It is to your benefit to get beyond rage, hurt, and betrayed. You want to end the relationship in a way that doesn't diminish them or you. You don't want to trash all the years you spent with them. Those years are a part of your life. And you don't want to part enemies, for it is a small world and you may want to have continued contact with them. When you just know that it is completed, you will want to wish them well as they continue their life journey.

> *The nature of divorce to get even is duplication;*
> *the nature of divorce as completion is expansion.*

To Do

You will want to be as generous as you can, about how you think about yourself and about how you think about them. It really doesn't make you feel lighter to carry around hatred. It festers, and you may find yourself many years after the divorce is final still feeling angry or hurt. You want to respect who you are and how you were about it. You want to look at them and at yourself with gentle eyes, realizing that placing blame doesn't really lighten it for you or for them.

Decide to stay married until you aren't.

Decide that you want the very best for yourself and for your partner.

Be smart where you can.

Be generous where you can.

Decide to remember the good times.

Count the learnings that you gained in the marriage.

Remember that you are not the story of your divorce.

Remember that good will is about you, as well as about them

*A
fundamental
misunderstanding
about*

Children

*is
that
they
aren't perfect.*

Imagine yourself living in a world of giants. Everywhere you are confronted with giant ideas to comprehend and giant tasks to complete. This is how the world seems to small children. More is asked of them in any given day than you yourself would be able to accomplish.

—You ask them to get themselves ready to leave in twenty minutes sharp. They hardly have the coordination to tie their shoes, and you want them to arrive at the door perfectly clean and tidy.

—You ask them to mind their manners perfectly when they go out with you. You strap them in a cart, for up to an hour of grocery shopping, with metal bars as their only cushion. You sometimes take them out when they are tired, hungry, hot, or cold, and then you scold them when they cry.

—You ask them to eat perfectly in ten minutes. They have one choice for dinner, and you decide it and how much. They didn't like the taste of it, and they were full when half of it was eaten.

—You ask them to cooperate when the relatives come to visit, and expect them to be perfect angels. But when they try to get your attention, you shoo them off like flies.

—You tell them "No" to almost everything that they would love to have or do. And you solicit perfect behavior with threats that would scare even you.

In fact, you expect them to obey the very rules that never worked for you. You want them to turn out perfectly and to be everything that you aren't, as they learn to grow and cope in a world that often seems unfriendly.

Children reflect perfectly your attitude when they are in your presence. They learn exactly how you do and replicate it as best they can. If you decide that they have little significance, they will demand your attention one way or another. If you decide that they are loving little creatures, your wish is their command. They listen to all your encounters, and repeat exactly what they hear. They adopt your attitudes with perfect accuracy. If you hate, they are hateful; if you are sad, they are anxious; if you are glad, they are happy; if you are angry, they are too. They are the givers of a great gift, which is to reflect who you are. Because they unconditionally forgive any and all of your inadequacies, they are perfectly flexible in how they feel about you. They will respond depending upon how you set the mood.

Choices

What children want from you is not so hard to fathom. They want to know that you approve of all they say or do. They hope to win you to their side for what else can they do? They are at your mercy; you teach and guide them how to be. Children have a perfect innocence until they learn better. They take everything literally until you prove it's just pretend. They are perfectly honest with what they understand.

It doesn't really matter if you have children or not. Their influence will be felt because they share your space. They are your nieces and nephews, your neighbors and your friends. When you are older, they will make the rules for you. They will be the doctors, lawyers, and politicians who will decide about the planet and its living conditions.

Children are the easiest people to love because of their innocence. They really don't know, and they really do want to learn. Every day of their life is like a new beginning. They can't imagine what the day has in store. They are about discovery because they always want to know more.

They can teach you how to dream and how to be alive. Their world bursts with amusement and awe as they joyfully run from one adventure to another. They are vulnerable, without the armor of mistrust and hate. They love you without reservation, and they tell the truth. You can count on children to be perfect, the best they have learned.

Wouldn't it have been wonderful if one person had thought you were perfect as a child? If, in your world of giants, someone, somewhere, knew you were trying to do your best? That you wanted more than anything the approval of those you admired? That you did your best to be perfect at everything you tried? That you just wanted everyone to love you and give you another chance? Wouldn't it have mattered more when you did succeed? You would have grown full of courage to be all that you could be.

> *The nature of childhood is trying;*
> *the nature of children is perfect.*

To Do

When you cherish children, you cherish life. Life begins with children and their indomitable spirit to make life perfect. Given a chance to please you they will, given a chance to admire you they do, and given a chance to love you they want to. And when you think a child is perfect, you will experience their perfection.

Teach a child one thing.

Tell the neighbors how you admire your child.

Send a card to the child next door.

Expect them to be adults only after they are.

Include them in your activities and your thoughts.

Do something they have always wanted to do next week.

Think twice about why you are apologizing for them.

Take them home when they are tired.

Give them boundaries that are about them.

Teach them to love by loving them.

Respect their efforts.

Acknowledge them.

Tell them you are glad they are a child.

*A
fundamental
misunderstanding
about*

Mothers

*is that
their only
job is
you.*

Mothers were people before they were mothers, and even they forget. Your mother softened your process even when you didn't know it. She held the pain and anguish of your life, as well as that of your siblings and of her own process of growth. She is a person with her own needs and all the personal concerns life presents to every individual. As a mother, her patience has been sorely tried, and she has been made wrong about everything and anything. But she copes.

Mothers continue to love you when you have done or been your worst. They are for you when no one else is. They still want you to be happy, and they have risked a lot to be on your side. They will help you out when everyone tells them not to. They still believe you'll make it, given one more chance. They are glad to see you, they rarely think you fail, they think you are the best looking, they think you have the most potential, they believe in you even when you don't.

No matter what you think about how she mothered, when you were born, your mother was thrown into a reality of the greatest joy she had ever felt as well as the greatest pain. She discovered how demanding mothering was on her energy. Her moments, her energy, her thoughts, and her concerns no longer seemed to be about herself. There was always you to be concerned about, to pay attention to, to do for. Your needs became her needs, and your desires became her desires. She gave to you when she couldn't, listened when she was distracted, cared when she was empty, and kept doing when she was exhausted.

Many times she wanted to quit, thinking she wasn't qualified, she had nothing left, she had done it all wrong, or you didn't care anyway. A myriad of feelings could sabotage her wonderful experience of mothering. She analyzed everything from A to Z, attempting to discover if she was doing it right. She wondered why she wasn't happier.

—She thought she had given you everything, and you weren't happy. Why wasn't she happy?

—She knew she loved you more than anyone, and you seemed not to care. Why wasn't she happy?

—She would give up her life for you, and you never said thanks about anything. Why wasn't she happy?

—She cared deeply and profoundly for you, and you told her to butt out. Why wasn't she happy?

Perhaps she was unhappy because she never learned to think enough of herself. It's ironic that you think she should have given more, and she thinks she gave all that she could. Maybe if she had told you "No," said, "Get someone else to do it," "I'm not available," or "Do it yourself," more often, she could have had her own great life. Perhaps she began to think that her life was only about your demands, and so did you. And if she did begin to get a life, allowing you to learn to be responsible for yourself, you grew up blaming your troubles on her absence. It's very easy to blame your mother. Many people agree—their mother wasn't there, didn't mother "right," didn't do enough, and ruined their life by imposing her values.

Choices

The truth is your mother wanted to do it right. She wanted to be your friend. She blessed the day you were born and has spent the rest of her life trying to bestow those blessings upon you. You will never find a better friend than your mother. She has years that she has invested in you. To be your mother carried with it her greatest challenge. Her hopes and dreams were for a family that was nourished and for you to grow into an individual who was loving and giving.

She never wanted you to have problems or to do

without, and she sacrificed many of her desires to give to you. And, in response,

—were you the best kid on the block?

—did you cooperate with others in the family?

—did you obey the rules?

—did you appreciate her attention?

—did you ask to help her?

—did you introduce her to your friends?

—did you expect her to do your chores?

—did you whine and complain?

—did you think you shouldn't have been punished when you didn't do what you were told?

—did you interrupt her when she was busy?

—did you call her names?

—did you talk to her like an enemy?

—did you take advantage of her generosity?

—did you blame her when things went wrong?

—were you nice to be around?

When you think about your mother, how generous are you? What do you expect from her? Why do you think that she is her very last concern, and what price do you think she has paid? If you want happiness for your mother, help her to think a new way.

Talk to her about herself, her needs, her desires, and those things that would make her happy. She has placed the condition for her happiness on your happiness long enough. She must live her life, just as you must live yours. Help her let go of you by communication and actions that tell her that you turned out and can take care of yourself.

The reward will be ease in your relationship. It won't be hard for her to let go of you when she has a life that is full.

---

*The nature of blaming your mother
is childish;
the nature of acknowledging your mother
is maturity.*

To Do

Mothering is one of the most significant jobs in life. And this job affects us all. Acknowledge mothers by considering them. Encourage and support them to remember themselves, and everyone will realize the rewards.

Ask your mother what she always wanted to do.

Consult with her about changes.

Tell her where you live.

Give her the good news.

Encourage her to get a life.

Ask her her opinion.

Tell her the best part about her mothering.

Tell her why you like her.

Return her phone calls.

Acknowledge her generosity.

Put up with her at least as much as she put up with you.

Be glad she is your mother.

A fundamental misunderstanding about

Fathers

is that they are not on your side.

People feel every way about their fathers. Some lucky people believe they have the best father in the world. Some feel their father is a stranger, or they have severed their relationship with him. Some are angry with him or blame their history on him, and others feel that their father never cared about them for one day of their life. If you don't think much of your father, you and he are losing.

Maybe you could feel more generous if you knew that he thinks providing for you *is* caring for you. It could be that he feels his contribution wasn't acknowledged or appreciated. His life has been directed toward fulfilling what he believed were his responsibilities.

—Maybe you could feel more generous if you knew that he did the best that he could.

—Maybe you could feel more generous if you look at your own kids.

—Maybe you could feel more generous if you remember your mistakes.

—Maybe you could feel more generous if you didn't have so many expectations.

—Maybe you could feel more generous if you knew that he didn't always know how to be.

It was difficult for him to know exactly what your expectations were but now he knows by your reaction that he didn't parent according to your favorite ideas.

—Maybe you expected him to have all of the answers. After all, he was the dad.

—Maybe you expected him to save the day, like a knight in shining armor.

—Maybe you never expected him to make mistakes. He was supposed to be strong and flawless.

—Maybe you expected him to be soft and gentle, but you were horrified when you saw him cry.

—Maybe you expected him to fix what was broken, and maybe he didn't know how.

—Maybe you expected him to fight your battles, and he made you stand on your own.

—Maybe you expected him to be a leader, and he hated competition.

There are as many images about fathers as there are children to create them. And whatever your expectations of him might be, what you really want is to *be* in relationship, because you already are. He is your father.

Choices

You want to have a relationship with your father as much for you as for him. Having black clouds about your father leaves you feeling done to and bitter. You both feel left out. To have a relationship with your father, you may have to start by including him in your life.

—Does it hurt you to let him give you advice? You can say, "Good idea, Dad," and do what you need.

—Does it hurt to call him for no reason at all? He may get the idea that you want something besides money.

—Does it hurt to tell him he taught you that you must do as you do? He wants to be proud that he made a contribution to your life.

—Does it hurt to contact him after he told you "No help" for your latest venture? Maybe he has wisdom because he has lived more of life.

—Does it hurt to forget your past differences and make the first move? He may have his own feelings of being done to.

—Does it hurt to include him on days other than Father's Day? He may want to know you, and have things to share.

—Does it hurt to tell him that you are glad he's your dad? Of all the fathers in the world, maybe he isn't so bad.

—Does it hurt to tell him that he is important to you? Maybe he feels bad that he didn't do more.

It's a big job being your father. He has his own pressure, his own feelings, his own insecurities, his own challenges, and you want more. He has always been expected to hide his troubles and settle yours.

Believe that he did the best that he could, whether it was what you wanted or not. Blaming him won't make your life better, and it could make it worse. You want your relationship with him just because of who he is to you. Give up your expectations, and you will discover that he isn't so bad.

> *The nature of being a father is biological;*
> *The nature of fathering is participation.*

To Do

Your father is forever. At the very least, he will be around in your thoughts. To settle your differences with your father means that you have outgrown your past. Your memories no longer control your feelings about him.

Tell him the most important thing you learned from him when you were a kid.

Share something that is hard for you to share.

Take him to work with you some morning.

Invite him to go someplace where he wants to go with you. Pay for it.

Give him your undivided attention when he is talking to you.

Think gentle about him.

Let him be exactly who he is.

Let him show you how to do something that he knows how to do.

Appreciate his time.

A fundamental misunderstanding about

Parents

is that your problem is their fault.

The thing about parents is that everyone has them. They are a part of you throughout your life. You probably have known and been in relationship with your parents all your life, although some have lost one or more parents and some never knew their birth parents. Perhaps you have step-parents or have long distance relationships with your parents, or even have severed your relationships with your parents. Others may consider them "best friends."

In every way, you are your parents. Their genetic structure fashioned yours. Their backgrounds gave you your background. Their lifestyle defines yours. Their values affect yours. Their beliefs undergird yours. As you have grown, perhaps you have rejected some of the beliefs and values that were so dear to your parents. Perhaps you have done so gently and respectfully, honoring your own life, and sharing it as you could with your parents. Perhaps you have done it with anger, resentful of the beliefs that you have lived with so long, asking your parents why they did as they did.

And inevitably as you look back at your childhood and through to your present, you judge your parent's parenting. You may think that

—they were the greatest parents in the world;

—they were abusive and unfeeling;

—they were too demanding;

—you lived in a dysfunctional family;

—they liked your siblings more than you;

—they neglected you.

Looking back, you may feel resentful and angry, or you may feel grateful for their love and support over the years. No matter what the specific feelings you have for your parents, these are the people who provided you with your care and your upbringing. When you really look at it, you know that they did what they thought best; they did what they could do; they did what they could, the best that they could. Did they not want the perfect life for you? When you are able to know inside that that is what they wanted to give you, you may be able to forgive and forget what they couldn't give. When you can give up reliving your awful childhood, year after year, you can look at your parents anew, with love and gratefulness for what they provided, and for who they are now.

The fact is that you are always their child, and they are always your parent. No matter the specifics of your childhood history, it is *your* history. It is one you cannot erase. However, it is one that you can embrace—one you can love.

Your parents are your history. If you evaluate them and your childhood as awful, if you reject and hate your life with them, you carry that into your present life. Real healing and love can take place only when you embrace all the parts of your life, even those that you consider unfair, unjust, and unlovable. All you really want to do is just love your parents, and you cannot while carrying around years and years of resentment.

Even so, as you continue to live out the childhood patterns, you may find yourself wondering, "Why is it that when I talk with my parents I still get crazed? Why is it that my parents have so many opinions about my life?" You may want to consider how you are presenting yourself to your parents. Are you presenting yourself as a mature grown-up or are you, in some ways, relating to them as you did when you were young? Are you and your parents easily making the transition from the early "I know best" role to "We live in the world together, and we are on each other's side"? As you present yourself as an adult to your parents, your relationship will take on new meaning. You will begin to see your parents as people living lives of their own, and they will begin to see you living your life.

Choices

Whatever the specifics, you likely will find yourself in the position of caring for your parents in one way or another. If you become the caretaker of your parents, you may find yourself in confusing situations. You may find yourself feeling different ways about it.

—You may be glad to be able to help your parents in their aging.

—You may be resentful, not wishing to give them any of your energy.

—You may feel bitter about having to provide for them financially.

—You may feel animosity at what you consider their impossible demands.

—You may feel you don't have the time, the money, the energy, the desire, the whatever to give to them.

The thing to decide is what do you want to feel about your parents? You are going to live the rest of your days with them one way or another. You are going to relate with them, directly or indirectly, for the rest of your life. Giving them what you want and what they need, making the decisions that need to be made will be difficult if you are caught up in the resentments and anger of "stuck" and "have-to."

The truth is that how you are and will be with your parents is about you. It is not about your parents. It is a choice you make about how you want to be. You want to be with your parents in the moments of life they are living. You want to live these moments of life in the way that you want to remember them.

—Are you going to feel good about you if you have a fight at Christmas, and don't talk with them again?

—Are you going to feel good about you if you neglect the responsibility once you have actually assumed it?

—Are you going to feel good about you if you take care of them with resentment and anger?

There is no guidebook written that describes how to live your specific life, including your life with your parents. But there is a guide within that leads you to be the way you want to be in the living of the moments.

The choice you make is part of your life. Embrace your role in the choices that must be made; they are about you. They are about how you want to live with yourself for the rest of your life.

You will want to make the choices that you respect yourself for, that you love yourself for, that you value yourself for. You will want to make choices about the moments that you have, knowing that you won't have these moments again. You will want to make choices, knowing that you are the one who has chosen. You will want to create with your parents the relationship that you want. You will want to be with your parents in the way that enhances everyone's life.

> *The nature of resenting your parents*
> *is resenting your past;*
> *the nature of taking pleasure in your parents*
> *is loving your present.*

To Do

Being in relationship with your parents through your entire life is about you. It is about how you want to be and how you want to remember your life. Live the moments as if they count, for they do.

Think of your parents' faults as eccentricities.

Claim all the parts of your history with your parents as perfect contributions to your life.

Listen to your parents' complaints without taking them personally.

Tell your parents what a significant contribution their life made to you.

Choose the responsibilities that you take on without resentments.

Make decisions about your parents' lives remembering that they are people too.

A fundamental misunderstanding about

Work

*is that
it is something
to do in
the meantime.*

One of the most familiar questions from childhood is, "What are you going to be when you grow up?" You are primed throughout your developmental years to think about, even dream about what you might be when you become an adult. You are encouraged to seek work that you are naturally drawn to, even work that excites you. You are led to believe that the work you choose for yourself can be interesting and fun.

After much thought and soul-searching, a path is chosen that often involves a great deal of special study in order to prepare you for this chosen work. Whether it is apprenticing in carpentry, taking courses in data processing, working your way from the stock room to a management position, or getting an MBA, you persevere through the highs and the lows in order to get yourself a job you can love.

At long last, the day finally arrives, and you begin in earnest the task of every adult—your work. At first it is enormously challenging, interesting, and exciting as you learn and perform the work you have been preparing for all your life. You get up in the morning eager. You feel a need to hurry up and get this job down so that you can feel a little self-assured about how you are preforming.

And you do learn the in's and out's of this job. You become quite skilled at it and feel at ease about handling the responsibilities given to you. Eventually, though, as you find yourself more comfortable and in familiar territory, a strange thing begins to happen—you find yourself getting bored. The work becomes more routine, and it is difficult to generate the enthusiasm that you once had for it. You begin to resent the fact that you have to get out of bed in the morning and get up for it.

—Maybe your expectations were too high about what you wanted to do when you grew up.

—Maybe people are right when they say that work is a necessary evil.

—Maybe it was a little odd that you enjoyed it so much; it must only have been the newness.

—Maybe you had tendencies of turning into a workaholic, so you decided only to put in your eight hours.

You begin to look around at the people you know and notice that not many of them seem to be happy in their work. You travel the streets or the railways on your way to and from your work and notice that you are one of the masses of people dragging themselves about because of the necessity to earn a living. Your major desire is to hurry and get done so that you can go home and watch TV. As a matter of fact, you spend a great deal of time dreaming of the day when you can rest and retire.

Wasn't there some point to it all? Can you really feel as though you are doing something useful, as opposed to something meaningless? The trouble with trashing your job or holding it as a necessary evil is that nearly one-third of your life is spent at this activity. It is difficult to isolate unhappiness to only eight hours of your day. Unhappiness in such a large chunk of your life has a tendency to spread like a virus throughout all the parts of your life. Is there a possibility of enjoying the many hours you must spend at work?

Choices

You are going to do something with your time. Somehow or other, you are going to spend your energy. You have an allotment of some unknown but limited number of days of your life, and you would like to think that you are spending this life energy to some purpose. When you take an honest look, the feeling of having made a contribution feels great. Even if your contribution is primarily in the quality of your own life, it counts.

Who decides when and what work is unpleasant? How much energy is too much to be spent at work? Who decides, whatever the task, how you are going to be *inside* about it? How many times are you going to make the coffee or go to the staff meeting being resentful that your time is being spent this way?

You can put in the time doing your work while you are begrudging it, or you can hold it as a contribution. Lightening up your own mood while you work is a gift. Have you ever noticed how your blue funk spreads to those around you?

The work must be done whether it is in your home or on the job. When you get that this is what is, choose how you want to be about it. You are in charge of the workings of your life; create it to be how it makes you feel good.

You are the one who determines the quality of your life work. If you are doing a work that you love, you feel rested. Remember how good it feels to get in bed after a good day's work, having that feeling of accomplishment? Find the things that you can derive satisfaction from, because you are the one who must live with dissatisfaction. Satisfaction is a matter of your creation; it is not dependent upon the details of the task. Even the most interesting job can be devoid of satisfaction if you do not choose to find it.

Remember that it feels great to succeed, so why not go the extra mile. Loving your life is a process of finding or creating lovability in all of its parts. And when you do experience loving your work, people notice you— you stand out as an example for others to see the possibility of loving their own lives.

> *The nature of resenting your work*
> *is tediousness;*
> *the nature of loving your work*
> *is satisfaction.*

To Do

To find the work you love is a matter of your willingness to find satisfaction in what you already do.

Decide to show up at work tomorrow with the intention of loving your day.

Think about how you can spend the allotment of energy for this day in a way that creates satisfaction, as opposed to boredom.

Notice the next time you are trashing your work and stop it.

Inventory the moments of your day before you go to sleep; find the times you created loving your life at work.

Go to work glad that you can.

Finish a project, and give yourself credit.

Tell someone at work why they are important to you.

Do something unexpected.

Do something extra.

Take your boss to lunch.

Learn one new thing each week.

Buy a new pen, and use it only at work.

Fix what is broken.

*A
fundamental
misunderstanding
about*

Money

*is that
it controls
the quality
of your life.*

So you don't have enough money to pay all the bills, give your kids money for lunch, travel, drive a reliable car, and all the other things that you think are necessary in your life. Short of winning the lottery, your chances of turning your financial picture around look pretty hopeless. Of course, if you did have more money, you would live in a better house, tell the boss off and quit your lousy job, leave them, be happy, and give your kids what they want.

Of all the issues of life, money is set off in a category of its own. Not only do you blame the scarcity of money for all your troubles, you actually don't like to do much about money in general.

—You don't like having to do the work you do to get it.

—You don't like balancing your check book, and all the other details of handling it.

—You don't like thinking about your money affairs.

—You don't like making plans about it, such as budgeting, savings, or retirement.

You have been going along struggling about money almost as if it were your enemy. How can you expect money to be a part of your life when the very subject darkens your mood? Could it be that all along you have been thinking that money is a necessary evil, when all it is is a means of exchanging energy?

Money was invented as an exchange of energy. In exchange for the energy it took to put a new wheel on your cart, you gave the wheelmaker fifty bags of grain that you grew on your farm. This bartering was a means of exchanging energy for goods.

Today, however, since money is a symbol once removed for energy spent, it is difficult to remember that it really is energy. The money that you have represents the energy of your thoughts, emotional desires, and physical labor.

Choices

What you need is a new way to think about money. All you want to do is live your life as magnificently as you can, and here your mind is blaming money for all the scarcity and trouble around you.

Money is not much different as an issue than all the other issues. You need to take money out of its special category and realize that things that work about other issues will work about money as well. If you feel that you are powerless about the issue of money in your life, you will be.

So let your mind imagine what life would be like if your ship came in with all the money you ever wanted. What would change? All the other issues would still be facing you. All the resentments, incompetencies, and even insecurities would still be there. And if your ship doesn't come in, you are still not powerless about these other issues.

—If you hate your job that much, change it. Don't blame money.

—If you must get out of an abusive relationship, do it. Don't blame money.

—If you hate the space you live in, fix it. Don't blame money.

—If you hate that you are always broke, make a plan about the money you do have. Don't blame money.

—If you are not happy, do something. Don't blame money.

As you begin to think of money as a form of expenditure of energy, look at how you can turn this energy into a positive experience in your mind. Start where you can.

Stop resenting all the things about handling money. Be glad that you can pay the bills or pay on the bills. Thinking resentfully only creates negativity about money. Instead, when you spend money, spend it where you really want to spend it. It makes you feel good.

Don't look back and trash your history about money. You know that you did the best you could at the time. Just think of money the same as you think of all the other issues of your life: your thoughts create what is about it. Be intentional about creating only positive energy around the use of your money.

> *The nature of scarcity is dependency;*
> *the nature of abundance is independence.*

To Do

Money, by its very nature, flows in and out of your life. When you understand that your thoughts directly facilitate or hamper this flow, you can become more careful about what you are thinking about money. Choose to think of yourself in charge as opposed to out of control about money energy.

Before sitting down to pay your bills, clear your mind of all the resentments about this.

Buy yourself something that you have been wanting, and notice what it does to your energy level.

Be gentle on yourself about your past dealings about money.

Decide where and when to spend your money.

Buy exactly what you want.

Make a list of what you have enough money for.

Buy one best item rather than two dozen second best.

A fundamental misunderstanding about

Burnout

is that the cause of it lies outside of you.

So how do you know when you are burned out? Are you feeling exhausted all the time, even when you get a good night's sleep? On the emotional level, do you find yourself depressed, frustrated, anxious, bored, apathetic, defensive, or hopeless? Do you take two weeks vacation and return to work only to find yourself as unenthusiastic as before you left?

Once you have looked at the symptoms and have done all you can to alleviate them and still feel burned out, you must look elsewhere. You may begin to see that the real issue of burnout is "becaming."

Becaming happens when you stop stretching. It is past tense; you notice that all the great stories of your life took place years ago. You look back longingly to some part of your history as the best years of your life.

Perhaps you became a lover, a lawyer, a parent, a teacher. After you became, it is hard to find an interest in anything. As a matter of fact, you can't remember when you last really got excited about something.

If you are having trouble deciding whether becaming is an issue in your life, the following inventory will help you get a sense of what is. Remember that this is just an exercise to find the red flags, not to judge yourself about it.

—Do you feel unappreciated, either at work or at home, with no one noticing all the effort you put in?

—Are you bored and finding yourself unable to get interested in anything?

—Are you emotionally exhausted, feeling as though you cannot bear to go through even one more small issue?

—Perhaps you feel you can't go any further; it's hopeless anyhow?

—Have you lost your passion for everything, even your favorite things?

—Maybe you have done it all and have no more goals in sight?

—Do you find yourself feeling misunderstood by your friends, your spouse, or your boss?

—Are you feeling drained and powerless and know that it is useless to fight city hall?

—Do you feel as if you have no life to call your own?

—Are you sick of the whole thing?

—Have you noticed that you can hardly get up for it?

—Do you have feelings of not being loved—that no one cares?

You can tell you are becaming at work when there are no more promotions to get or jobs that interest you, you have been passed by for promotion five times, and the closer you get on the drive to work the heavier you are.

You can tell when you are becaming in your primary relationship when you allow the worst of yourself to show up there, when you are bored and want to move on, when you have memorized the TV guide: if it's *Sixty Minutes*, it must be Sunday.

You can tell when you are becaming with your family when you wait until the last minute to prepare for family events, when you resent having to do all the gift buying, when you don't want to see their faces anymore.

You can tell if you are becaming in your social life when you keep trying to get out of engagements with friends, you breathe a sigh of relief when the last guest leaves, you can't find anything interesting in conversations.

You can tell you are becaming in your spiritual life when nothing moves you, you don't feel connected to anything, there is an emptiness in your life.

You are either becoming or you are becaming. There is no coasting. Becaming is from the inside out; your light burns out. What you feel is dead.

—Becaming is contagious to other people. Have you ever noticed how one person's bad mood can take a whole group down?

—Becaming spreads to all areas of your life. It's difficult to be miserable for eight hours and be up for the rest of the day.

—Becaming is boring. You are bored, and you are boring.

—Becaming is numb, in a stupor, mesmerized, hypnotized, roboticized.

—Also, becaming is the universe trying to get your attention. The universe is telling you:

> *It is done.* You have done marriage counseling or have gotten the promotion, and there is nothing left—no real problems to work out, no energy there.
>
> *It is broken.* Things simply aren't working.
>
> *It is used up.* You have outgrown the circumstances. You have gotten what there is to get in your growth and development.
>
> *It is full.* It is like a bucket filled to the brim and unable to take another drop.
>
> *It is out of balance.* You have put out all this time, creativity, and energy, everything you've got, and there is nothing coming back.
>
> *It doesn't count with you anymore.* You have lost the passion for it. There is nothing about it. You just don't want it in your space anymore.

Take a moment and consider where the universe is trying to get your attention. Putting your attention on these areas can move you along in your personal evolution and assist you in not being done with your life before you are dead.

If you notice that you are becaming, it is an opportunity to gather a little energy to get on with the life you were created to live. The universe may be telling you that your mission in life is not complete. Nobody was born for nothing, even when you find yourself coasting in life as if you have nothing to do on this planet. It is time to get on with your living.

Choices

In order to get beyond burnout, you have to get into the place of becoming. And, in order to do that, you must make a decision in favor of your own personal evolution. Evolution is still happening in your life, but you must choose it. You can get your becoming going again. Be bold in your wanting. When was the last time you were bold? Bold is an active word, not passive. It means that you have to mobilize something. It means doing what you need to do even if you think it is too risky. When you dig in your heels and say "No, I'm not going to do this one," that might have been the very one that would have kicked you over into becoming again. Boldness is not just about twenty-year-olds. Boldness is about evolution. Boldness is about your life becoming.

When was the last time you allowed yourself to want something? You know that a want is a wish, and a wish is energy. When you want it badly enough, you are willing to do what it takes to create it. Truly, you can count on wanting; it will provide energy to accomplish the task. Sometimes we forget about wanting or even feel a little guilty about wanting things. Wanting is part of becoming. If you want to be the best darn teacher in the world, guess what? You have a shot at it. If you don't *want* it, you might as well forget it. You won't tap into that energy of evolution.

Be alive in your life. You want to get the light inside turned on and get movement. You want to take on your life as a project—much like you took on creating a home to live in or starting your own business. Say to yourself, "I want life in my life." This is now your issue; it's your project to look here. You know that there are moments when you have done this—when you have turned this on for yourself as a conscious act of a human being creating their life. It is not an accident that some people are more alive than others. If you want to be alive in your life, you must create becoming.

Trust in your knowing. There are things that you know about your life that you don't have logic and rationale behind. Have confidence in that; trust it even though there is no reason logically to do so. If you trust in it and let it guide you, if you move where this knowing suggests, you have the possibility of moving along to a lighter, bigger life. To be in the process of becoming, you must have confidence in your knowing.

Another thing that will kick in your becoming again is to say, "Yes." Some people have a rule in their life that when something new is proposed, they automatically say "No." That way they can think about it and not make a rash statement. However, an automatic no can stop you dead. Movement is about saying yes. And saying yes is gutsy. When you say yes, you get yourself out there where you are not sure you can even do it. How many accomplishments have you had that, at the outset, looked undoable? No is about becoming; yes is about becoming and your personal evolution.

> *The nature of becaming is dissolution;*
> *the nature of becoming is evolution.*

To Do

In order to get beyond burnout you need to begin to hold your whole life, and everything in it, as the most important thing for you to be doing and for you to be thinking about. The work of your lifetime is your own life; it's your own personal journey. When you do this, you can recapture those feelings you used to have about setting the world on fire. You knew you could. You knew that your life could make a difference on this planet. That's when you were becoming.

Decide that you will make an honest appraisal of the extent of burnout in your life.

Take a dream that you have always had, and be bold in wanting it.

The next time an opportunity comes to stretch yourself beyond what you thought you could do, say "Yes, I'll do it," even though you don't know how at the moment.

Take something that you know about your life, even though you can't explain it rationally, and decide to go with it and watch where it leads you.

Apply for the position you always wanted.

Lose twenty pounds.

Make new goals. Include your real passions.

Decide where you will be one year from now, and do what it takes.

Fix up your environment.

Invite people to a party, and tell them your new plans.

Mastering

A fundamental misunderstanding
about mastering
is that
it isn't possible.

Mastering

You already know that you were born a unique individual. No one is just like you, and no one has lived the life you have lived. Not one other person has an identical nature or can know your nature more than your ability to translate your experience. No matter how hard you try, you cannot clone yourself after any other person because you cannot live the life they have lived. Your values and beliefs have been your impetus for defining your reality. You've had input from guardians, teachers, and experiences that taught you, and from this you have learned what you value and what you don't.

Sometimes while you are in the midst of your life content, you are forced to review and change your beliefs. Your present values or beliefs may not be applicable to what you want to do now, so you discard the beliefs that are standing in your way. Other times you can't get to where you want to go with your present values or beliefs so you look for new ones that will give you the permission you need to make the moves you want to make. All the while that you are adding to and subtracting from your values and beliefs, perhaps you fail to notice the subtle changes that are taking place.

—Some things you said you would never do, you are doing.

—Someone you thought you couldn't live without has disappeared from your thoughts.

—Some things you thought you could never accomplish, you have achieved.

—Some habits are forgotten.

—Somethings you were once grateful for have turned sour.

—Some dramas are now funny stories.

You may be a person who feels serious about life, a person who feels positive about life, or a person who manages life, and you want values that fit who you believe you are. You want life to fit the reality that you have defined for yourself. Most often, if you continue to choose toward lightness, it does. But sometimes, while you are trying to manipulate your reality, you will find yourself again involved in familiar territory that you have been trying to escape, or your living will take you into new territories that startle you.

—The debilitating problems that you severed your old relationship to solve may now appear in your new relationship.

—The harassments you left your old job to escape may now appear in your new job.

—The self-doubt you thought you conquered may appear with this new challenge.

You may find yourself shaken up, shattered, and tossed about with each new drama that life presents to you until you wonder what you can believe, what you do value, and what is real?

While you are pausing to wonder what is happening, nature is working. Seasons are changing, creating the reality of spring or fall or life or death. Nature's way is also applicable to you. It is guiding you toward a new, natural reality which, once discovered, is a reality recognizable as the one you were born to live. And when you discover your natural reality, about any given issue, you will have mastered what life has always wanted you to know.

You can choose to live the reality that is a natural condition for you—a condition that nature is always working to expose. There is a reality of perfect harmony about your life that is naturally demanding alignment. If you choose alignment, what you will experience is mastery and a new way to live. Things will matter to you that didn't matter before, and things that did matter will begin to matter less or not at all. Items that you never considered as possibilities before will seem natural to you.

—Naturally you would want to love not hate.

—Naturally you would want to succeed not fail.

—Naturally you would want to forgive not begrudge.

—Naturally you would want to contribute not hold out.

—Naturally you would want abundance not scarcity.

Nature's way demands that you master living in harmony with your natural condition. And nature doesn't make it difficult. Your resistance to living and choosing what is real for you is what is difficult.

When you align with your natural condition, you ultimately will discover life is easier on you because you begin mastering its content. Although the new content may be radically different from what was when you began your journey, you are in harmony with the reality that has been present all along. Nature is on your side, so listen carefully, see clearly, and be thankful that you are mastering its process.

A fundamental misunderstanding about

Your Story

is that it is the worst, the best, the most interesting, or the most tragic that has ever happened.

Naturally, you want to share the details of your life. Some details you can't wait to tell to all of your interested parties. Other details you save for certain people. Some of the best ones you hold for the critical moment to share and others you share to get them off your chest. You tell your stories for a lot of reasons.

—You want sympathy so you tell the story of your abuse to anyone who will listen.

—You need excuses for the mess you find yourself in, and you have a tragic childhood story to blame it on.

—You feel they will understand why you can't be relied on when they know the stories of how you were used.

—You think you should tell them how awful your past relationship was so they will never do the same to you.

—Your stories of close calls keep everyone entertained at the parties you attend.

—You think that you will be popular with them when you tell the latest six stories of your accomplishments.

—You tell your stories because you want to impress someone special.

—You tell your stories because there isn't anything else for you to talk about.

Most of the time you don't consider your motivations for telling your stories. They are about you, and that's your favorite subject. It makes you feel better when you can corner someone and keep them entertained with all of the colorful details of your story.

When you sense you are losing their attention, you ask a few questions like, "You know what I mean? Don't you agree? What do you think? Can you understand?" Before they can respond, you have taken off on another story to drive your point home. But do you share the stories of your life in a way that the telling of them makes a difference to you or to others?

Occasionally, you tell your story and you notice they are moved by it. In turn you notice that something happened to you in the process of telling it. You and they have had an experience that will not soon be forgotten.

It would be a wonder if something you wanted to share actually made a difference by your sharing it. You have a lifetime of opportunities to talk with others, to be influential, and to be influenced by personal stories. You experience great life-worth when your dramas make a difference to someone. You don't have to write an article for *Reader's Digest* to be acknowledged for living the content you have lived. What you do need to think about are ways that you can share intentionally what you have lived.

Choices

Whether your most recent favorite story is funny, sad, educational, scary, or tragic, there is value in how you live what you live. An experience can actually take place for you and your listener when you choose to share your event with a purpose. If you are sharing complacently, your stories are worthless because you don't really care about them and neither do they. Told randomly, your stories may bore, insult, anger, outrage, or diminish. Told intentionally from caring, your stories can heal, empower, inspire, and educate.

Sharing with others is an important investment. You don't always know when they will take you seriously or when they will think you are a fool. What makes the difference is your motivation.

Your stories are unique to you because you have lived them. What you what to share more than the details of your story is what you have experienced as you lived it. You want to share how the event altered your reality—what the event made you think about you and your relationship to your world.

The significance of the story is in the effect it had on you as a human, living a human life. Others have compassion for humanness. They appreciate that you have lived through it and have become happier, wiser, more peaceful, or successful because that is what they are searching for themselves. They can identify with you.

And when you create an experience with them, sharing your story may be their teacher, their catalyst, their motivator, or their healer. Your story might save them learning time because they can change a collision course. Your story might heal their pain because someone has gone through it and survived. Your story might give them new information because they didn't know it could be done.

Also, they are looking for others that will share their stories because they are looking for permission. The very story you tell might be the one that they have kept a secret. Your telling it gives them courage to unburden themselves. Go ahead and share the stories of your life. Simply shift the manner in which you are sharing them, and they will make all the difference to you and to them.

> *The nature of random stories is irrelevancy; the nature of intentional stories is teaching.*

To Do

Make a commitment to yourself to share your stories to make a difference to the listener. When you do, you are the benefactor. You are pressed to tell the story in a way that interests you. You already know the details because you were there. What you can glean from telling your story has to do with you.

Before you share your story, make sure you have their attention.

When you have their attention, tell the story with the intention to hear yourself tell it.

Tell the appropriate story at the appropriate time.

Tell the story to create an experience.

Tell your story when you are ready to make a difference to yourself and to them.

*A
fundamental
misunderstanding
about*

Consideration

*is that you can
give them what
you cannot
give yourself.*

Sometimes it is difficult to think of yourself and your desires and needs when you are involved in relationships. You feel a responsibility to think about your spouse, children, parents, neighbors, and colleagues and the demands they make upon you with their needs and wants. It can be confusing to determine when your consideration of them directly interferes with your creation of your life.

You probably spend a lot of your time involved with responsibilities you feel toward others. You think about and experience their problems, you think about and experience their desires, you think about and experience their successes. At times you notice that they are doing fine while you are confused and wondering why you are feeling so desperate about your own happiness. You have been involved in their life for so many years you can no longer think of what you need or want. You may begin to notice a slight edge of resentment.

—You worked to put them through school and now they graduate and tell you that you are not stimulating enough for them.

—You have been superparent for your kids, because you know how you want them to turn out. Now they are old enough to have turned out already, but you still find yourself hoping they will.

—Perhaps you have spent the last twenty-four months respecting your supervisors, staying late without being asked, doing little things to make their life easier, and they pass you over for that promotion.

—And you didn't neglect your parents. You have taken them in to live with you, saving them from a nursing home. You run their errands, drive them around, cancel your life when they can no longer care for themselves. And they spend their time telling your neighbors how wonderful and successful your sister in Chattanooga is.

In some of the best cases, you get the gold watch for your efforts. Most times, others don't really notice or appreciate your sacrifice. They begin to believe you owe it to them, or think you can't do anything other than be there for them. They forget that there is a person living your life—one that wants and needs to be considered.

If only you could conquer that nagging feeling of wondering when you will get your needs fulfilled. If you cannot conquer that feeling, you might consider what is really going on with you.

—Perhaps you consider them first because you are afraid not to. They know where you are vulnerable, and you don't want to cope with their threats.

—Perhaps you consider them first because it has become a lifetime habit. You have always been this way, and now you feel powerless to do it any other way.

—Perhaps you consider them first because you don't think you have needs anyway. You should feel rewarded enough by the privilege of serving them.

—Perhaps you consider them first because you believe there will be something in it for you. You are keeping track of what they owe you, and you are planning to demand payment.

It is fine to consider others first when you really can. Consider them freely, with no charge and no expectations. However, it is not easy to consider them first when you are an empty vessel. Let them help fill you by telling them your hidden needs, by explaining that you need rewards and acknowledgments.

The issue is not to deceive or deprive anyone, you or them. The issue is knowing yourself and others well enough so that everyone gets what they need. You must give to yourself first until you no longer need to, and then you will long to give to them.

The paradox is that sometimes it is selfish to consider yourself first, sometimes it is selfish to consider yourself last, sometimes it is selfish to consider yourself at all, and sometimes it is selfish if you are not your primary consideration.

Choices

All of your life, your *self* has given you secret messages about you for your consideration. Your *self* would like your attention, your approval, and your encouragement. Your *self* is not any different than some other favorite person you have.

When you love a brand new baby or a brand new lover, what do you want for them? You want them to have a great life that they love. Wouldn't that include having things and situations in their life that enhance the uniqueness of their life? Wouldn't you hope that they could have it all? Parents just want their children to grow and be happy. Lovers say about their loves, "I just want them to be happy."

The relationships in your life reflect how you feel about your *self* and your life. They let you know if you have taken time to consider what nourishes you, what fills you up, what turns you on. They reflect if you deny your *self's* needs and desires, or if you criticize and chastise your *self*. At the least give your *self* a break. Give your *self* the benefit of the doubt. Give your *self* one more chance. You are the important person here—the one that needs your attention. Your *self* won't care if you get that big promotion if you aren't doing it for you. Your *self* won't care if your home runs smoothly if you sacrifice you to make that happen.

Others will not care about your dreams if you don't care. They will not be happy with you if you are not happy with you. They will not be caring or loving if you are not caring and loving your *self*. They will agree with what you think and feel about your *self*. You will see their agreement in how they are and what they do. Likewise, whatever you are thinking about your *self* is reflected in what you are thinking about them.

You can fool your *self* about your needs not mattering for only so long. The longer you are not happy with you, the more resentment you experience when you must give them what you cannot give your *self*.

The nature of self-rejection is resentment; the nature of self-consideration is wisdom.

A Matter of Choice

To Do

To have a life that you love waking up to, get up honoring your *self* and the day that you are about to live. Your *self* wants your participation in your life. It wants you to consider what you want to do. And it wants you to give your *self* attention so you can get on with it. Give everything to your *self* that you want to give to others. Then you will notice that you are full, and what you do will make a difference in the lives of others.

Start the project you have always dreamed about.

Buy something because you want it, needed or not.

Get up early to begin your day how you want.

Fix what you like for dinner one day a week.

Start back to school with one class next semester.

Take a day off, and play golf.

Fix a space just for you.

Try something new for fun.

Allow yourself mistakes.

Rest when you need to.

A fundamental misunderstanding about

Expectations

is that they help you figure things out.

Expectations are notions you have about a particular outcome. They seem to help you know something about the future—you think that you wouldn't know what to decide or what goals to set for yourself if you didn't expect results. So you continue to have expectations about many issues and for many reasons, even though they often don't materialize according to your plan.

—You expect them to do what they say they will do, but they don't.

—You expect to get the promotion when you give your all, and you don't.

—You expect your kids to turn out because you sacrifice, and you're not sure they are.

—You expect good health because you gave up bad habits, and now you have a problem.

—You expect that you handled it once and for all, and now you are thinking about it again.

—You expect yourself to behave now that you know better, and you are doing it again.

—You expect that you won't make a fool of yourself, and you do.

—You expect them to love you forever, and they aren't.

—You expect them to have your right answers, and they are wrong.

—You expect that you have found the solution, and you haven't.

—You expect them to be what you want them to be, and they won't.

—You expect it to be a certain way, and it isn't.

—You expect them to be a certain way, and they aren't.

—You expect that you have found some answers, and you haven't.

—You expected that life would get better when you accomplished X,Y and Z, and it hasn't.

Expectations are baffling when what you do expect doesn't happen, and what you didn't expect does happen. Sometimes you expect the worst to happen and it does, and sometimes, instead, something great happens. Or you expect the most to happen from the least, and the least happens from the most. It is very difficult to know what to expect, and it is scary to think that you might or might not get what you expect. How then are you supposed to make plans, to know what to do, to understand your life, to know to whom or where to turn?

Choices

The nature of expectations isn't so mysterious when you think of them as restrictions—as limitations on what it is possible for you to have in your life. Life cannot deliver miracles or perfectly fulfill your wants and desires if your expectations have delineated the only solutions you can accept. If only your expectations are fulfilled, you must settle for what you get.

When you *give* something expecting something, *change* something expecting something, or *do* something expecting something, you will often be disappointed. The disappointment comes from the fact that people and situations cannot be counted on to meet your expectations, exactly as you've planned.

Expectations are your illusion about the future. They are what you have when you have forgotten about living in the moment. If you live and plan your life expecting particular outcomes, when they don't come through exactly as you expected, you may blame the misfortune on someone or something else. Foiled expectations give you excuses not to take responsibility—you won't have to take the blame because you expected it to be different, and you're not taking credit because you don't recognize the possibilities in unexpected outcomes.

However, when you are living in the moment, without expectations, you know exactly what choices to make. You don't have to have expectations because you are there, choosing what you want right then. When you give, change, do, adopt, adapt, or share, simply because you want to, you are taking responsibility for your life. You don't do it for some hidden or obvious expectation that may or may not be fulfilled.

> *The nature of expectations is illusion;*
> *The nature of living in the moment is real.*

To Do

Give because you want to not because you'll get something or be rewarded. Choose to do those things and to be those ways that make you feel good about you. When you make choices that are concerned with your present circumstances and what you want, you have no expectations about the outcome. Continue to plan and do and think big about your future, but make your decisions based on your present—because you want to, rather than because you expect something.

Decide to be in relationship today because you want to.

Decide to continue the program you are enrolled in because you want to.

Decide to give them a gift because you want to.

Decide to lend them money because you want to.

Decide to be good to yourself today because you want to.

Decide to choose in their favor because you want to.

Decide to choose in your favor because you want to.

Decide to look for the best in your life because you want to.

Decide to be conscious of your environment because you want to.

Decide to give up a habit because you want to.

A fundamental misunderstanding about

Decisions

*is that
one
is
enough.*

Decision making is not always a welcome activity, especially if it seems like yours often stick you with unpleasant repercussions. Decisions have been blamed for everything from the worst event in your life to the best event in your life. Perhaps you have learned to approach decision making with more caution than you would use to enter a war zone.

The trouble with decisions is that they never go away. Every day someone or something requires you to make decisions. And most decisions have consequences. You decide on one position, and it seems to ripple throughout your universe. The bigger the decision, the bigger the ripple. There have been times that those ripples have turned into tidal waves, and you would like to avoid that at all costs.

You have gathered evidence about decisions, and you think it best to avoid them. Therefore you try to limit yourself to tiny decisions—ones that can't possibly cause too much trouble. You only deal with the kind that won't cause ripples, the kind that really won't make a difference in your life.

If this is true, it means that you have made big decisions about decision making. And right or wrong, the reasons for your position often come true.

—Maybe you fear decision making and have decided that you don't make good decisions.

—Maybe you have been criticized once too many times about decisions that you made.

—Maybe you think there is a better decision to make, and you are waiting for it to show up.

—Maybe every time you make a decision, things get worse.

—Maybe you hate to make decisions because you fear that you will have to live with the consequences.

—Maybe decisions make you crazy because there are too many choices.

—Maybe you gave up making decisions because someone else makes better ones than you do.

What you need to know is that n̲o̲t̲ making decisions about your life gives someone else control. At best, life gets dull and uneventful when you refuse to make decisions. At its worst, life gets unbearable when others control and manipulate you, because, assuredly, they will be happy to make your decisions for you.

Not making decisions communicates to others that you are not capable—that they shouldn't expect much from you. They will come to rely on the fact that you just go along with whatever they decide about your life, whether you like it or not. You won't have to do much, and you won't have much to do.

Not making decisions keeps you stuck. And not making decisions creates a small life to live. If you are tired of the life you have or any part of it, you may be avoiding decision making.

Choices

Take another look at decisions because they can give you the personal power that you long for. Consider that decisions are just decisions. A decision is just one choice you make of many that you have. When you realize that, you have more options. Go ahead and make that decision, and if it doesn't take you where you want to go, make another one. In fact, make lots of decisions. Decisions are what get movement into your life. If you are tired of the same old thing day in and day out, maybe you are not making enough decisions.

The more decisions you make, the more you will want to make. Make many decisions every day, and it will become contagious. Decisions are your ally when you make the ones that are on your side. They can be your great motivator. They inspire you because they get you into the life you want to live.

> *The nature of indecision is stuck;*
> *the nature of decision is movement.*

To Do

It's always your choice to make decisions. Life naturally presents you with decisions to make about every facet of your life. Embrace them, and they will help you fulfill your dreams.

Ask for fewer opinions rather than more when you need to decide.

Decide in your best interest.

Make the decision sooner not later.

Write down your options and pick one.

Don't judge your decisions, past or present.

Make decisions that expand rather than contract.

Make decisions that feel lighter to you.

Make a decision about your job.

Make a decision about having children.

Make a decision about money.

Make a decision about your relationship.

Make a decision that includes.

Make a decision that empowers you.

Make a decision to make many decisions.

If you don't like your decision, make another one.

*A
fundamental
misunderstanding
about*

Habits

*is that
you recognize
one when
you see one.*

No one wants to be accused of having bad habits but we all do. What you think of as your bad habits probably are, and some things about you that you don't even consider as habits probably are too. There are subtle habits impacting your life that you have never noticed. You may have been busy living and wondering why you don't get your due without ever considering that maybe it's because of some of your habits.

—Perhaps you have habits that get you a reputation for being the world's worst critic. You spend your time looking for the worst, and you find it.

—Perhaps you have habits that make you look fragile. You communicate that you aren't very capable, and they believe you.

—Perhaps you have habits of never feeling good so they don't bother to ask how you are anymore.

—Perhaps you have habits of being moody so they never know what to expect.

—Perhaps you have habits of saying "No," so they don't invite you much anymore.

—Perhaps you have habits of pointing out their flaws so they don't want to share much with you anymore.

—Perhaps you have habits of nagging, and they turn you off and tune you out. You can't get your point across anymore.

—Perhaps you have habits of complaining, and they retreat when they see you coming. They don't want their day ruined.

—Perhaps you have habits of withdrawing when there are difficulties to meet. They have felt rejected by you once too often, and they rarely call.

—Perhaps you have habits of being late, and they don't wait for you anymore.

—Perhaps you have habits of coloring the truth, and they don't believe you anymore.

—Perhaps you have habits of quitting when the going gets tough, and they tell others not to count on you.

—Perhaps you have habits of manipulating, controlling, whining, depressing, and wheeling-dealing. Maybe your habits include resisting, bragging, and showing off.

The trouble with all of these habits is the life-altering designs that they influence. You want to be one way in life, but your habits have shaped a different life for you.

Going the direction you know you were meant to go in life will require that you become aware of your habits. Once recognized, you can get your habits under control. You can make decisions not from habit, but from choice. It is a liberating experience to know that you can make choices for your life, including the choice not to align with your habits.

Choices

A good way to begin to master habits is to collect some that enhance your life. Make it a habit to think positive thoughts in your favor. Your habits originated in your thoughts, so give birth to habits that you want.

You want habits that will empower you, so think that you can. You want habits that will bring you success, so think that you are. You want habits that give you peace of mind, so think thoughts that settle you. You want habits that bring you good fortune, so think that you have it.

If you need support to expand your life and redirect your course, identify and become master of your life-altering habits. Your reality will change with the change in your habits. You will have greater success because your old habits are not in control. You—the person with choices—will be running your show.

> *The nature of bad habits is many problems; the nature of good habits is fewer problems.*

To Do

Half of the battle is won when you identify your habits. When you catch yourself in the act, you can do something about them.

Identify your habits.

Catch yourself indulging, and choose if you want to say or do that.

Wake up tomorrow determined to notice your chronic behavior. Say "Ah ha!" when you do.

Acknowledge yourself when you see your pattern changing.

Make it a rule to think positively about yourself.

Give yourself a gift when you succeed, and don't be hard on yourself when you don't.

Tell someone else that you intend to give up your most offensive habit. Tell them why.

Begin today.

A fundamental misunderstanding about

Thoughts

is that no one knows your secrets.

Recall the many times that you were thinking of someone and two minutes later they called you on the phone. And remember those times that you were thinking something and the person you were with suddenly said it. Or, what about the times that they knew your thoughts about something when you were trying to keep them a secret. You can't remember telling them what you thought, and you wonder how they knew.

Here all this time you have been going around thinking any old thoughts about everyone and everything expecting that they were your private thoughts. If they are so private, what explains how others know something is wrong when you are telling them everything is all right? If others are catching your simple thoughts, what about all your other thoughts?

If it occurred to you that they know what you are thinking, how much trouble do you think you would be creating with the present thoughts you are having? Actually, how much trouble *are* you creating with your thoughts?

—When you are late and you are thinking how angry they will be when you arrive, how angry are they?

—When you just know that they will be upset because you forgot to call, how upset are they?

—When you do something that you believe they will disapprove of, how much do they disapprove?

—When you purchase something and just know they will hate it, how much do they hate it?

Sometimes it appears that you know how they will respond because you know them so well, and they always respond that way. And then one time they don't respond as you knew they would. You remember that you had something else on your mind; you forgot to think about how they would respond. Suddenly, they have responded to your being late by feeling bad for you being caught in traffic. The tone of the entire event unfolds opposite of your previous assumptions.

What about the times you don't want them to know something, so you concentrate on keeping that information to yourself. But when you have attention on the secret you are keeping, they know something is up, even if they don't know what. They make accusations, and you get defensive. They get hints and you deny, and soon you are caught in an unpleasant situation.

Doesn't it seem strange how information that is not relevant never comes up for discussion, but now that you have information that you don't want discussed, they are prying into your secret thoughts relentlessly? Isn't all this curious? Doesn't it make you wonder about cause and effect? Could it be that your thoughts about how it is are creating the situations?

Choices

Thoughts have energy and the strength of their energy is the same strength with which they affect you and others. If you don't want information spread via the cosmic grapevine, don't give those thoughts energy with your emotions. The more you try to hide your thoughts or keep them from another, the more guilty or suspicious you are. The more you expect a habitual response, the more you will receive it. Try thinking something else, and see if they respond differently. Try thinking that they are on your side, not against you. Try thinking that they won't disbelieve that you were caught in traffic. Don't assume they will be jealous, angry, hurt, or distant; maybe they won't be.

This is the manner in which your thoughts contribute to your experience of your relationships and your life. Fortunately, you have the option to think for yourself about yourself and your life. Some things have to do with another, and some don't. If you don't want to arouse their suspicion, then make the secret information irrelevant in your own thoughts.

Your thoughts contribute to the creation of your relationship and their response to you. When you want them to be on your side, assume that they will be. What you think about them and your relationship with them will come true. Living life and creating great relationships requires that you think what you want and want what you think. They know about you and your thoughts. You communicate to them in every way. Your secret thoughts are often the ones that cause you the most trouble. You can't fake it, they will know—you can't suppress it, they will know. What you can do is live your life reflecting your love and caring, and talk to them with your thoughts in the manner that enhances how you feel about them. Your life is more of an open book than you may have suspected. When you leave the book open for others to read, be determined to have them read what you want them to know.

> *The nature of careless thoughts*
> *is assumptions;*
> *the nature of focused thoughts*
> *is reflections.*

To Do

The cosmic grapevine is always at work helping to reflect your thoughts to you. You will get a clear picture of what your thoughts create by the way your world reacts to you. Fortunately, you can choose to think what you want to think, and you will want to think about others in a way that supports your creating with them what is important.

With your thoughts, tell the person who is angry that you would like to solve the differences between you.

With your thoughts, talk to your children and explain your concerns and hopes about those issues they don't want to discuss with you.

With your thoughts, ask them to call when they are late.

With your thoughts, ask for understanding.

With your thoughts, forgive them.

With your thoughts, send them good will.

With your thoughts, ask them to forgive you.

With your thoughts, picture reconciliation.

With your thoughts, approve of them.

With your thoughts, ask them not to fault you.

With your thoughts, tell a person you love how much they mean to you and how much you understand.

*A
fundamental
misunderstanding
about*

Commitment

*is that
they will
because they
made one.*

It is not news that life has no guarantees, but we still try to get guarantees by making commitments. Guarantees seem to create safety. You make commitments of every nature in relationships. Some large and some small. Sometimes you make itemized contracts to insure that you will get and give exactly what you want, or that the love you experience now will maintain your relationship forever. Sometimes you make commitments lightly because you believe that no one can be trusted anyway. Or you make commitments that you hadn't even considered as "commitments."

—You make commitments to share your life forever, but you hadn't expected them to change.

—You make commitments to be faithful, but they don't understand you.

—You make commitments to be honest, but you don't count white lies.

—You make commitments to take care of your family financially, but they want the divorce.

—You make commitments to help them advance their career, but you can't be expected to move there.

—You make commitments to honor them but you think they are always wrong.

It is not always easy to fulfill a commitment, especially one that is forever. When the going gets tough, it is often easier to make justifications to break your commitments than to honor them. After all, things change; they have changed; it's not what you expected. Determine what your position in your relationship is. Are you waiting for it to be over, or are you in it for the duration?

A commitment is only as reliable as the moments you create together. They may be prepared to pay the price of severing their commitment with you. They might believe that it is less costly to pay the price of leaving than to pay the price of staying.

Choices

When you want them to be in relationship with you forever, your moments with them need to add up to "I will." When you realize that you influence their ability to keep their commitment to you alive, you won't set out to make it impossible for them to keep their commitment.

—People tend to fulfill their commitments to you when they love their relationship with you. They don't want to let you down or to injure the relationship.

—People tend to fulfill their commitments to you when they know you appreciate them and that you don't take life with them for granted. They enjoy the joy you find in them.

—People tend to fulfill their commitments to you when they know you are on the side of yes in your relationship. They will live through many things with you if they know you are working toward "It's a go."

—People tend to fulfill their commitments to you when you basically like them. They can tell by your interactions with them if you are on their side or not.

—People tend to fulfill their commitments to you when more of your moments add up to I will than I won't.

People can and do endure many things. They have issues that involve you and some that don't. Participate in the ones that involve you, and care about the ones that don't. When each is for the other, you are on the side of creating forever with your commitments.

> *The nature of uncommitted is isolation;*
> *the nature of committed is connected.*

To Do

When you make commitments to another, you are really making commitments to yourself. You are making a statement that you can count on you, which indicates that they can count on you. No matter where you are in the process of life, you can be on the side of yes with your commitments. No matter the difficulties that you encounter, you have a commitment to yourself to see it through. When you experience that you fulfill your commitments, you are willing to be challenged, to be vunerable, and to do many more things.

Do one thing that will make it easier for them.

When you tell them you will help them, do it.

Resolve to not keep track of their mistakes.

Give them a day off.

Take their needs seriously.

When you tell them you are for them, be for them.

Do a project together.

Dream and make plans together.

Appreciate them.

*A
fundamental
misunderstanding
about*

Sexual Energy

*is that
it can only
be expended
by having sex.*

Energy can be defined as your personal potency. Sometimes it seems like a strange force charting its own course, demanding your attention. Your knowledge of it includes knowing when you are tired and have low energy, or if you are drained by the energy of emotion, or if you are stimulated by mental energy. And you can tell if you are experiencing the sensation of sexual energy.

Many times the energy of sex is the strongest energy to manage because it is a uniquely powerful energy that draws your attention in many ways. You may find yourself being affected physically, emotionally, and mentally by the attention sexual energy sometimes demands. When sexual energy surfaces, you make choices. You use it many ways for many reasons.

—Perhaps you use sexual energy as a distraction in your life.

—Perhaps you expend energy sexually to avoid being responsible for your life.

—Perhaps you use sexual energy to satisfy a longing to be loved.

—Perhaps you use sexual energy hoping to say something important about yourself.

—Perhaps you use it to lure others into believing what you don't.

—Perhaps you use it to cover up what you know about you that you don't want them to know.

If you believe that sexual energy is only about sex, you have forgotten that this is an energy of motion. You can recognize the presence of motion or the absence of motion. Sometimes motion has no direction; it runs rampant, and you feel out of control. There are times motion is tightly controlled, and you feel depressed and exhausted. Other times motion is directed, and you experience your desires fully.

Sexual energy is a core energy of motion. It is an agent for your expression. You have found yourself expressing your sexual energy in many ways. Often when you are required to expend your energy with intense physical activity, you do not expend your energy sexually. Some feelings, such as depression, interfere with sexual expression. And your mental attitude plays a role in your ability to use this energy. There are many possibilities for sexual energy, and having sex is only one.

Choices

There are times that sex consumes your thinking. You think about it, you see it everywhere, and you are constantly aroused. Sometimes you have available all the sex you want but it continues to absorb your thoughts. It can become a menace by its persistence, pervading your thoughts, consuming your energy, and controlling your actions. Left unchecked, it becomes your ruler.

But you have choices about the way you use your sexual energy. This energy is for more than sex. It is for creating motion in all aspects of your life. When you find yourself unsatisfied, regardless of how much sex you have in your life, it is a clue that you are wanting something more. Channeling your sexual energy requires that you inventory your life to discover what wants to move. Channeling the energy of motion is an ongoing process. It happens day by day, project by project, and idea by idea. It happens when you channel or focus your personal power to give voice to your passion and make movement toward its inception.

When sexual energy is used with intention and integrity, it is the energy of your personal power and passion. Personal power is your ability to be of influence when you contribute, and passion is your most profound desire.

You will be the director of this powerful energy and determine how it influences your life. If you have thought that you can only experience passion sexually, you are limiting your creative expression. Give yourself some space to be the director of your life. Use your energy to have sex, yes, but also learn to use your energy to fulfill all of your dreams.

---

*The nature of one expression of sexual energy is sexual potency;
the nature of many expressions of sexual energy is creation.*

To Do

When you want to be intimate with another, express your passion sexually. If you do not or cannot be intimate with another, find another passion for the expression of this energy. The most important thing about this energy is that it requires consistent expenditure toward some passion.

Make a list of your passions.

Use your energy to know your *self*.

Use your energy to get a new idea.

Use your energy to meet a current challenge.

Use your energy to make new plans.

Use your energy to manifest your goals.

Use your energy to empower others.

Use your energy for recreation.

Use all of your energy every day.

A fundamental misunderstanding about

Manifesting

*is
that it
happens
by accident.*

When you get something that you have wanted, do you hold it as good luck, or that you were blessed, or that it was obviously supposed to be? And when you don't get what you want, do you believe that you probably weren't supposed to have it anyway, or that your luck ran out? Have you ever wondered why some people never get what they want, and others seem to get everything they want? This is no accident. Getting what you want is about manifesting—about making it happen.

What gets in the way of your getting what you want?

—Do you find it hard to decide what it is that you *do* want?

—Do you think that you should want only the things that you really need?

—Are you confused about what your needs are?

—Do you feel that you must justify anything you get, and wanting isn't justification enough?

—Are you sure you can't hold onto what it is that you want long enough to make it happen?

—Do you believe that there is something a little selfish about the whole idea of wanting?

—Or, perhaps, the last time you really wanted something, it caused so much trouble that by the time you got it you didn't even want it anymore.

Before you can set out to deliberately manifest something in your life, you have to get OK with wanting. The act of wanting is simply the act of focusing your energy in a particular direction. It generally arises out of a need, whether that be on the physical, emotional, mental, or spiritual level.

For instance, a need for rest and relaxation may lead to wanting a vacation. If it is below zero outside and you know that nothing short of a week on a sunny beach will do, then that is the want to focus on. A weekend off puttering around the house will not satisfy this need. At this point your mind usually kicks in and starts to list all the reasons why you can't manifest a vacation. It will tell you that you can't afford it, and that it is a frivolous idea. This is what the mind does.

If you really want to begin manifesting things in your life, you must begin to take your wants seriously. Assume that your wants do not arise for nothing—for this is, in fact, the case. Imagine what would happen if you did not take the more obvious wants, such as food, water, and sleep, seriously. It doesn't come up in your mind to question these wants, and you do everything you can to fulfill them. You are totally focused about this. But as soon as wanting gets beyond pure survival, you take your wants less seriously. And the further from survival your wants are, the less credence you give them.

Choices

Wanting is focusing the energy of need. When you can focus clearly on what is wanted, the things to do to make it manifest will show up. At each step along the way, you will be at choice about doing what it takes. The strength of your wanting will dictate whether it manifests or not. And each moment that you allow yourself to waver in your wanting is a setback to manifesting. The magnitude of your ability to manifest is a reflection of the strength of your want. If you want it badly enough, you will do what it takes to make it happen. That is the only secret there is.

So, for instance, if you *want* it to have made a difference that you have lived this life, consider

—How strong is your need to make a difference?

—Is this something that you really want to do?

—Have you considered what it will take to accomplish this?

—Are you ready, willing, and able to do whatever it takes?

—Are you intentional about supervising your mind's activities in order to prevent setbacks from negative thinking?

People who have mastered the art of manifesting have learned to notice their needs and honor their wants. They understand that doing all the details is essential to the outcome. And they rely on the energy inherent in their desire to sustain them until what they want is accomplished.

> *The nature of not wanting is a void;*
> *the nature of manifesting is fulfillment.*

To Do

Your ability to manifest is dependent upon your choices, not your circumstances. The slightest doubt about this fact will have a direct negative impact upon manifesting. Mastery is a belief before it is a fact.

Make an inventory of your present needs.

Look and see what your beliefs are about wanting.

Identify something you have been wanting, and tell someone that you are going to manifest it.

State a want and make a list of all the things that come up to do about it.

Notice what happens when you become intentional about doing what it takes.

Think of a time that you got what you wanted, and count that you manifested it.

*A
fundamental
misunderstanding
about*

Success

*is that
you don't
have
any.*

To be successful is a natural desire, regardless of the circumstances of your life. As you have lived your life, you have been noticing and accumulating different ideas about what success means. Your parents had ideas about it, and so do your significant other, your friends, your social group, the media. Some of these ideas you have set as goals for yourself, but sometimes what they want for you is not what you want. If you don't define carefully, you can find yourself striving for someone else's idea of success.

As a child you felt success when you took your first step, tied your first bow, got home by curfew, won your first prize, got a good grade, got your first date, got your driver's license, and graduated. As an adult, you felt success when you got married, had a child, landed your first job, got a promotion, built a house, won an award, or made a million.

You may notice the string of successes in your life and see them as milestones. You may wish that you had more of them, more often. And, reviewing them, you may wonder why, if you have had so many successes, you don't always feel successful?

The key is that success is a personal thing. It is about how you count your life as you live it. What is it that you define as "success"? If you don't live up to your own personal definition of success, you will never experience success, no matter how big the trophy at the end of the race.

—Perhaps you search for success in material acquisitions: the right kind of car, the right address, the right size house, the perfect art collection, or the fluid bank account.

—You may look in more personal ways: being the perfect size, wearing designer clothes, driving the big deal car, or having the newest and the latest whatever.

—You may desire and define success from relationships: with a significant other, with children, with co-workers and bosses, with friends, and with the community.

—Or you may seek success in status and influence:

getting a promotion, having a title, winning an election, having your picture in the newspaper, being a leader in the community.

If you only count as success those academy award experiences, you will not experience yourself as successful. If you only notice those red-letter days, you won't experience all the other days and experiences. However success lives in experiencing. As long as success is considered a thought or a feeling, it will continue to be elusive in your life. Success is experienced in the moments of your living. Success is the accomplishment of what one sets out to do with their energy in any given day.

Choices

Success is about courage. You can't think to courage, you can only go for it. Courage is not just moments on the battlefield. Courage is starting when you don't want to, are afraid to, can't, or don't know how. Courage is to do the work of the day—confronting difficult issues, talking to those you need to talk to, making the telephone call, or speaking up when you should.

Success is also about surrender. It means giving over to the personal wisdom that you have, without any guarantee of the outcome. Personal wisdom is what you know that you don't know that you know. It gets you through when all else fails. When you surrender, you say, "I'll do it," not knowing how you will.

And, success is about perseverance. Perseverance is coming to choice about the use of your energy for the day. You will use it in a way that enables you to experience success in your living, or you won't. You may have noticed that when you are the busiest, you accomplish the most. You have more energy. You don't want to grit your teeth through your life, but you do want to persevere—to be intentional, to go on, to go through, to not give up, to not quit.

When you look to your experience of living the days of your life, you will experience your successful *self*. You will genuinely know your life as successful, as meaningful, as worthwhile. When you are successful, who you are on the inside will match who you are on the outside.

Success is a personal thing, lived moment by moment—day by day. It is found in using your personal allotment of energy for each day, following your personal wisdom. Live your uniqueness, and in this uniqueness you will find your success.

> *The nature of unsuccessful is in your criticism; the nature of successful is in your definition.*

To Do

You don't want your experience of success to be limited to the top ten days of your thousands. So look in each day for your experience, and count the successes you find there. There will be more energy for you to become who you were meant to be, to accomplish what you were meant to accomplish.

Each evening review your use of your allotment of energy, and count those things that you did that you intended to do.

Do the thing you don't want to do, can't do, won't do, and never did before.

Inventory your ideas of success, and claim those that are yours as yours.

Notice in the moment those moments when you are genuinely successful.

Share with another the experiences of success in your day.

Choose this day not to expend your energy on confusion, anxiety, anger, indecision, and depression, and notice what happens.

*A
fundamental
misunderstanding
about*

Miracles

*is that
they
rarely
happen.*

A miracle is a gift from an unexpected source that arrives just in the nick of time to make a difference in your life. You may think there is a mystery about miracles, or that miracles happen for others but never for you. You might want miracles in your life but don't think you deserve them.

There are many positions about miracles. Some people believe miracles happen regularly for them. And others feel that they had one miracle, and they can't have anymore. Some positions are tied to religious beliefs, some are tied to luck, and some are tied to esoteric phenomena. But miracles happen in free space. When all else has failed, miracles often happen. They happen because they can, because there is nothing in their way. Have you gotten out of the way of your miracles?

When you want miracles, remember that

—miracles happen when you least expect them. Can you allow the unexpected in your life?

—miracles happen when all of your external efforts can't produce the result. Can you choose the way of least struggle?

—miracles come from different sources. What avenues do you refuse to explore?

—miracles are not what you think. Do you ever quit thinking?

—miracles are sometimes in opposition to your belief systems. Do you value your beliefs more than miracles?

—miracles enhance your life. Can you allow it to turn out for the best?

—miracles get you in touch with the unknown. Must you always have control?

—miracles do not have limits. What are your rules?

—miracles happen all of the time. What have you missed?

—miracles teach you something. Do you already know everything?

—miracles happen whether you believe in them or not. What do you give credibility to?

—miracles are natural. Are you suspicious?

—miracles create an experience. Are you timid?

Choices

If you wonder why you don't have miracles in your life, it may be that you never anticipate miracles. Perhaps you live your life with everything under control so you don't need miracles or you live your life out of control and expect that nothing of value ever comes your way. When you are living with a prescribed formula or an edited script there is little room to anticipate a miracle. And there is almost no room for change.

Miracles change the event, they save the day, they make the impossible possible. Creating space in your life for miracles is a consideration. You will begin to live with space to be guided, you will listen to your quiet voice. Miracles rarely shout your name to get your attention. They wait patiently until you give up. They wait until you become quiet and still and let go, knowing that things will turn out. They wait until you will accept the unacceptable. Miracles are waiting to happen in your life if only you can get out of their way.

> *The nature of luck is happenstance;*
> *the nature of miracles is alignment.*

To Do

A miracle can and does affect your life profoundly. You will need to create room in your life for miracles. And you will need to embrace the concept that your life can and will be touched by miracles.

Expect miracles.

Specifically define what miracle you need.

Give up your attachment to a particular outcome.

Position yourself to accept a miracle.

Get prepared for a change.

Do six things in the direction of the miracle you want.

Believe that you can, and do what you want the miracle to do.

The fundamental misunderstanding about

Cooperation

*is that
you
must give
up something.*

Cooperation is something you have been asked for many times in your life. They have appealed to you for your cooperation from the time you could first understand the language. And usually, it's about something they want from you. Your experience proves they only asked you to cooperate about details that you dislike. It seems that they don't want to do it, so they pass it on to you disguised as cooperation. Or it's something they don't want you to do, so they pass it on to you disguised as cooperation. Through the years you have had a lot of experiences with cooperation, and now it seems like a nuisance you might like to avoid. Why should you cooperate when

— you disagree with them?

—you won't get anything anyway?

—it's not your problem?

—you never wanted to get involved?

—they never appreciate you?

—it requires more from you than you can get in return?

—the last time you did they took advantage of you?

—your time is too valuable?

—it wasn't your mistake?

—you don't plan to stay anyway?

—you don't even like them?

—you didn't start it?

The last time you cooperated you got no satisfaction. They got what they wanted, and you felt used once again. Now if you come to agreement, they must cooperate with you. You have demands that must be met before you will give in. The time has come to have it your way, and you are prepared to prove it. Besides, do they take you for a fool? You notice that they have it all, and you are still having to struggle.

Choices

Cooperation is not the trouble. Cooperation is the foundation of agreement. The more you can come to agreement, the more everyone will get what they want. The problem with saying no to cooperation is that you get less, rather than more. You are limiting your options while thinking that you are limiting your troubles. Fulfilling your needs and desires takes all the help you can get. You need them on your side, and they need you on theirs.

When you find yourself in opposition, think a new way. What you want is to find the way that everyone can say yes. Your resistance might be the result of decisions you made very early in life that have little to do with the reality of now. If you cooperated before and it didn't work out, it might be because it was coercion not cooperation.

Perhaps you acted from resentment or from seeking approval rather than agreement. If fear of not getting your due is your particular concern, genuine cooperation has a lot to offer you. You get some of what you want, and you give some of what they want. You are living on this planet with billions of others who have their own wants and needs. From your family to the global village, you will be asked to team up. You will want to unite with them so you can contribute, and they will want to unite with you so they can contribute. What you get for your efforts is pleasure in their pleasure, thankfulness for peace, appreciation for their acknowledgement, gratitude for their concern, and most of all love for yourself and others because you are not alone.

> *The nature of opposition is hostility;*
> *the nature of cooperation is unity.*

To Do

You want to cooperate so you can be on the side of your *self.* You know that you have to live in close proximity with folks having every position about every subject. This closeness will necessitate some kind of agreement to enable you to live without personal concern. Cooperation will give you at least less trouble, and at best, will promote peace.

Make it a point that everyone says yes before you quit.

Give up one more point than you think you can.

Before you say no, be sure you know the long range ramifications.

Listen carefully to their position; they may be in agreement.

Find a new premise to the old issue.

Make it important to you only if it is important to you.

Try taking a different position.

Know what you want, and know what they want.

Think about it.

*A
fundamental
misunderstanding
about*

Being Human

*is that
they
aren't
trying.*

Out of the billions of people on this planet, you know that you are unique. It is easy to walk down the street and see others as more than you, less than you, different from you, other than you. But the one thing that you share is that you were born human. It is not easy being human. Much is expected of you; you expect much of others.

More than anything, you want to do your life perfectly. You want to have personal integrity and self-worth, great and loving relationships, and enormous success in a work that you love. You know in your heart that you want to hurt no one; that you want to bring peace, not anger; that you want to bring love, not hate; that you want to live your life each moment as perfectly as those peak moments that you have experienced, those moments when you have been generous, accepting, loving, contributing.

And you make mistakes. You misjudge. You act impulsively. You hurt others. You are your own greatest critic.

—You feel like a failure in your relationships and your work. You lose faith in yourself and in your abilities.

—You look back at an incident in your life ten years ago and wonder why you did it as you did. If only you had known then what you know now.

—You look in your present life and think if only you were smarter, kinder, more patient, more loving, more generous, more whatever, then you could consider yourself a good and successful human.

The reality is that you find yourself confronting people and situations. You hurt your most significant others, they hurt you; the kids make you crazy, you make the kids crazy; you insult your neighbors, they insult you; your friends betray you, you betray them. And other humans do the same things. They mess things up. They know when they do. You don't have to point it out to them. They, like you, are their own judges and juries. They are doing and thinking the same things. They are caught in all the pains and anger and disappointments that you are, in similar dramas with different characters. Being born human requires that you do all the human living. Every single thing happens to humans, and you are required to go through it. You experience the life that you live because that is your legacy as a human.

You know about human life: there is no perfect way to live it, and we all share in this living. Being human is about finding your own integrity and realizing that others are searching for their own as well. They too want to do it as perfectly as you want to do it. They are searching for the pure and flawless ways to be. The quest for the great life is one you share. You and they are doing the best that you can in living the human life in which you find yourself. No one decides to be the worst case they can be. Everyone stretches to be the best.

Choices

As humans we can affect people in insignificant passing ways, and we can affect people in profound transformative ways. Choose the way you want to affect the human condition. You make a difference in that condition.

—It counts that you smile at people, let the other car into traffic, help someone fix a flat tire, speak to the waitress, and talk with others in the grocery line.

—It counts that you remember birthdays as the celebration of a life, that you give food to someone who has none, that you give your attention to someone wanting to talk.

—It counts that when you see some other's pain, you are willing to hold their hand for a while.

—It counts that you are generous when you can be, loving when you are able, and helpful when you are capable.

—It counts that you include rather than exclude people.

If you remember your common bond of humanness, you will be less tempted to criticize, hurt, ridicule, ignore, or judge others. You will live with more compassion for others' lives. You never know when their dramas will become your's. You never know when you will experience the pain that they are experiencing.

The experiences of others' humanness affects you in many unseen ways. As one human being is in pain, so you are being influenced, and the overall condition of the planet is being created. You have already seen, in large and small ways, the effects of negativity. Look now for the effect you wish to make on the human condition.

The world is now accessible as a global village, and you will want to learn ways to live closer and more peacefully with others. Lighten up about them, and you will have more compassion for your own life as well. You can be glad to be alive, and to be sharing the human experience with others. The stakes are too high not to embrace the whole of humanity.

> *The nature of humans is trying;*
> *the nature of humanness is perfect.*

To Do

Human beings are caretakers of life as it exists on this planet, and each choice you make brings with it the energy of contribution or destruction. When you realize that you, as an individual, affect the quality and the continuance of life, you will want to be deliberate. You will want to make a difference wherever you can, in large and in small ways. Someone has to start. Let it be you.

Decide to live in a clean and healthy environment by choosing to recycle, to not litter, to do what you know to do.

Choose not to shout obscenities at other drivers, no matter what they do.

When you look at others, remember they are doing what they can.

Give your attention to those who need it.

Think the best about the ones that you love to think the worst about.

Choose to light your candle in the darkness so that others may see.

*A
fundamental
misunderstanding
about*

Good Will

*is that
it begins
with
them.*

When you greet the people in your life with "Good morning" or "Good day," you may want to see if you are also "Good willing" them. You will know the times that you aren't, the times you are holding them with less than good will. For example, how are you holding

—the driver that cut you off?

—the spouse who betrayed you?

—the neighbor kid who trespassed?

—the boss who fired you?

—the teacher who pressed you?

—the sibling who fought with you?

—the parent who demanded from you?

Sometimes these are small irritations that disappear in a short amount of time. By the time you got to work, perhaps you stopped fuming about the driver that you cursed on the freeway.

Sometimes these are gaping wounds that fester and don't heal, are easily opened with the next encounter, and leave scars. It may be that ten years after the divorce-you-didn't-want occurred, you are still carrying around anger for the person.

Sometimes these are hidden wounds. You carry them around, secretly tucked away. They were unfaithful to you once, and you say that everything is OK when you know inside that it is not. You are still resentful about what they did, and you want them to pay in some way. It is so easy in life to be self-righteous, hypocritical, insincere, or smug. You may often feel justified in being angry, resentful, hateful, or revengeful. When you are, you do not have good will.

The real question is how good do you feel running around mired in ill will? It jumps about your mind all the time, demanding that you remain upset and angry. It sometimes insists that you do something about it, like confronting the person or ignoring the person or arranging your life so you never have to see the person again. Sometimes ill will happens on accident. They weren't trying to hurt you, and you got hurt. And now you are harboring ill will.

—You may find yourself wishing that the person would get what they deserve.

—You may find your mind nagging you constantly, creating sleepless nights, anxious days, and sometimes ulcers.

—You may find that you are the only one upset and angry. They are going about living their life quite fine while you are consumed with rage.

—You may find that you continue to hold ill will for someone who is dead, resenting them for their life or for their death, and living out your life as a monument to that resentment.

When you find yourself acting in ways that lead others to question your good will, you may want to clear it up before it escalates into ill will. When someone's actions seem calculated to hurt you, you may want to choose not to take it personally, not to pick up those feelings of ill will that go with it.

Choices

By having good will, you have nothing to lose but negative energy. Holding ill will for people takes your time and energy hostage; holding good will for people frees you. When you have good will, you communicate it in ways that matter to you and to others.

—Good will with the significant others in your life creates loving relationships.

—Good will with friends creates a support system.

—Good will with co-workers creates cooperation and success.

—Good will in your community creates safety.

—Good will in the world creates peace.

Good will is a position you have about others in the world. It is a position that acknowledges the humanness of the human condition. It makes strangers less strange. When you have good will for another, you wish the best for them. Good will is a deliberate act, an act of intention and willingness. It is a state of being that you offer to others and the world. It is an act the world cannot live without.

> *The nature of ill will is enemies;*
> *the nature of good will is friends.*

To Do

You want to hold good will for all the people in your life, in all the ways they are in your life. Harboring ill will ultimately affects the quality of your life. It imprisons you.

Decide that you will not get angry with Y about some one thing that you always get angry with Y about.

Decide that you will not be crazed in rush hour traffic, no matter what they do.

Choose to think a different way about a person who hurt you in the past and who, in the activities of your mind, continues to hurt you.

Notice those niggling thoughts of ill will that you have, and stop thinking one of them.

*A
fundamental
misunderstanding
about*

Thankful

*is that
you can't
be until
it's better.*

You have read many books that tell you to think positively, but life is sometimes so complex that it is difficult to do. You would like to feel thankful, but things just aren't working out. How can you be thankful when it's all wrong?

—You can't be thankful when you don't have enough money. No matter how much you make, it is never enough.

—You can't be thankful when they left you. You forgot that you weren't happy when they were there.

—You can't be thankful when they pick on you. You don't understand why they don't understand.

—You can't be thankful when you just lost your job. You always hated what you were doing, but you needed that job.

—And you can't be thankful because your car broke down, you caught the flu, six people aren't speaking to you, you can't pay your bills, your kids drive you crazy, there is too much pressure at work, you can't count on anyone to help you, and you don't deserve any of it.

You find it difficult to have a positive attitude when others ask how you are. Instantly, you drop into all of the misery about your life. You portray yourself as the person that is always worse off. You talk about your problems as if they are sacred to you. You tell them what you think, what you feel, what it does, what you can't, why you won't. It gives you an excuse to stay right where you are, because you believe that your problem is less painful than the solution that is needed.

Choices

The day will come when even you can't stand it anymore. You don't like being the person that has all the bad news. However, there is light at the end of the tunnel. When you are ready, you will change what is true. Simply start with what you have, and be thankful.

They haven't been telling you to think positively for no reason. Consider your best problem and all that it means to you. You identify with your feelings about it, you tell others that this problem makes you helpless, it makes you inferior, it makes you crazy, or it makes you depressed. It, at least, gives you something to share when you can't identify your worth.

You can glean from your favorite problems what it is you can do. What if they thought you had enough money, didn't mind where you are, loved where you lived, liked your kids, were happy in relationship, didn't work too hard, had time for yourself, felt good, or had great days? This would provoke a whole new reaction from those who know you.

—They would count on you because they wouldn't feel that they were imposing yet one more thing.

—They would wonder why you are so happy now.

—They would see you as someone who could cope and had something to offer.

—They would tell others that you were special because you love what you do.

—You would be an example of successful living and be a positive influence on their thinking.

Being thankful isn't difficult when you choose to focus on your haves, not your have-nots. Being thankful for all things creates a state of mind that is positive. Being thankful is about looking for the best that you already have. So what if your mind wants you to believe that you don't have enough. You will never have enough as long as you think you don't. It's like a disease that spreads if you don't treat it.

To break the cycle you must make a different choice. You will see that when you focus on thankful, you will be more positive, which will, in turn, create more positive. When you are thankful for what you have, your reality automatically begins to change. It's imperative to look for the best, and soon that will be all you can see.

> *The nature of thankless is scarcity;*
> *the nature of thankful is abundance.*

To Do

You are the only one who can change your life from one of misery to one that you love. Being thankful is just as easy to do as not. You know how to focus, because you have already been focusing on what you don't have and receiving a lot more of what you don't want. Refocusing to thankfulness will change your life. It will bring you a lot more to be thankful for.

Be thankful that they live with you.

Be thankful for your friends.

Be thankful you aren't hungry.

Be thankful you are strong.

Be thankful you have a mind.

Be thankful you live today.

Be thankful you have another chance.

Be thankful you were able to pay the rent.

Be thankful you have a job.

Be thankful you got a promotion.

Be thankful someone loves you.

Be thankful that one thing turned out.

Be thankful you don't have to do thirteen ever again.

Begin and end your day being thankful for something.

*A
fundamental
misunderstanding
about*

Getting Wiser

> *is that
> you can
> forget what
> you know.*

On your journey through life, you probably went through a trauma or two that woke you up and turned your world upside down. Maybe you were forced to get wiser when you weren't ready to learn that what is true for you wasn't true for them. Things that you never wanted to think about, you had to think about—such as how to support yourself when you got laid off. Perhaps forces beyond your control had you doing things you never desired to do, such as learning how to meet the opposite sex when you were divorced after fifteen years of marriage.

And there wasn't much consolation as you grew, matured or evolved and went through a never-ending stream of events that pressed you to your limit. Sometimes you probably didn't want to know what you knew. You didn't want to live what you discovered. And you would have liked to stop the whole process and foget the whole thing.

Still, after the initial struggle, you emerged a new person, one much wiser and much braver. Recalling the process, you know how much more capable you are now. You learned to think for yourself and make choices that are in your best interest. You discovered that life bears the meaning that *you* attach to it. You figured out what is important to you.

You realized the importance of cleaning up your act, which you did gladly. You experienced the benefits of not having people shrouded with black clouds following you around. You patched up, worked out, and completed issues that had hampered your ability to live joyfully. Life has been satisfying; except for the fact that you expected it would get better and stay better when you chose to live awake. You thought that once you got on top of it you would have that smooth sailing called happiness. But you notice life keeps happening. Parts of your life no longer fit once change occurred.

—The friends that you enjoyed complaining with disappeared after you made the choice to look for the good about your life.

—The job was no longer applicable because you wanted to spend your hours working where it mattered to you.

—Some family members you were better able to communicate with, but others wanted no part of your growth and declared you a little weird.

—You figured out how you need to think or act about a situation this week, and by next week the circumstances are a wreck again.

—You worked it out with them, so why do they want to quit with you?

—You managed to get your debts current, so how could you be behind again?

—Why are they still relating to the old you when you want them to relate to the new you?

Why didn't someone tell you that the going would get rougher and the stakes would get higher? So here you are stuck, wanting out, wanting a few moments of peace, wanting the world to go away so you can collect yourself.

What you should know is that universally people want to quit, slow down, take a break, or give up altogether. They were happier for awhile but this new challenge doesn't seem worthwhile. They would rather not know all the time; it was easier to be ignorant.

Choices

It's difficult to notice when you are in the middle of your current process that it is all happening for a reason. However, you do have hindsight that might give you insight. Looking back, you know that working it out made it right for you. You even thanked your lucky stars that you learned what you did. You could never have lived through what you lived through without self-discovery, which gave you self-reliance. You have to admit to yourself that those old parties, those old friends, that old job, that abusive relationship, the indebtedness, all of the old black clouds don't fit who you are anymore. They don't interest you, and they don't empower you.

It's natural to fantasize that it would be better to go back to your ordinary life, where "victim," "circumstance," and "random" were key words in your vocabulary. But deep inside you know that the only way out of the present dilemma is through. On the other side is still a lighter you, a you that you will appreciate more and that you will know more deeply.

Simply and honestly put, you can't go back. You cannot live a pretense. Your growth has become a habit of living openly and vulnerably. Perhaps you have begun to view the bright side of life, and you have forgotten what the world back in your other life is really like.

—You have forgotten that they didn't care much, because you didn't care much.

—You have forgotten that you felt neglected, abused, misused, misunderstood, taken for granted, taken for a fool, rejected, criticized, lied to, lied about, and it all gave you ulcers.

—You have forgotten that gossip was a favorite pastime, arguing was a favorite way to get your point across, manipulation got you your way, threats were a way of life.

—People put up with you, you had a job that you outgrew, you had relationships that were phony, and you were the one that wanted to move on to bigger and better things.

You can't go back. Don't blame your process—you know too much. You have lived where others have not. You have started on a quest and, once begun, the way back disappears. The old familiar life gets strange. You see a reality that they do not. You left that life behind because it didn't fit for you anymore. You wanted to get to someplace else. Be thankful you can't go back. There isn't anything there for you. You would be an alien in a strange land, not knowing how to cope.

While continuing on your quest has difficulties and challenges, it also promises rewards. Those less experienced in life can learn from you, they appreciate you, they admire you. They encourage you to be all you can be by their faith in you.

But it isn't them that matters so much. Once you have begun there isn't anything else for you to do. Every time you surrender, you reach a new reality—one that begins to fit like no other. Then you remember why you started on this quest, and give thanks that you have come so far.

> *The nature of your old reality is fantasy;*
> *the nature of your present reality is what is.*

To Do

Finding a new reality, a new way to live your life may not be easy, but it is necessary. The times of your life indicate when you need to continue on your quest. You can continue under protest, or you can surrender. However you choose, going on is your only option if you want to continue to experience living. Going back is not an option because you can't be something you aren't, and your growth has taken you into a reality that doesn't exist back there.

Get up tomorrow being thankful that you know what you know.

Go to sleep tonight happy that you were privileged to live this day.

Keep positive thoughts in the forefront of your mind.

Smile when a less knowledgeable person can't.

You can, again and again and again, always choosing it.

Remember there are others worse off than you.

Embrace the life that you have.

Share with someone what you know.

Call an old friend to see what you still have in common.

Go on when it is hard.

Enroll others in your reality.

Be as much as you are.

Concluding

Index of Fundamental Misunderstandings

A fundamental misunderstanding about

Approval _____ 79
   is that your pointing out where
   they are wrong empowers them.

Arguing _____ 125
   is that you can win something.

Being Human _____ 293
   is that they aren't trying.

Blame _____ 59
   is that blaming them
   makes you right.

Burnout _____ 207
   is that the cause of it
   lies outside of you.

Caring _____ 117
   is that they determine
   how you care.

Change _____ 41
   is that if things change
   they will be better or worse.

A Matter of Choice

A fundamental misunderstanding about

Children ——————————————— 169
    is that they aren't perfect.

Choosing ——————————————— 15
    is that you shouldn't
    choose for yourself.

Commitment ——————————————— 259
    is that they will
    because they made one.

Communication ——————————————— 53
    is that what you communicated
    is what you meant.

Consideration ——————————————— 229
    is that you can give them
    what you cannot give yourself.

Content ——————————————— 111
    is that you know what will happen.

Cooperation ——————————————— 287
    is that you must give up something.

Decisions ——————————————— 241
    is that one is enough.

Divorce ——————————————— 163
    is that when it's over, it's over.

A fundamental misunderstanding about

Expectations —————————————— 235
    is that they help you
    figure things out.

Falling In Love ———————————— 147
    is that it is always what you think.

Fathers ——————————————————— 181
    is that they are not on your side.

Fear ————————————————————— 75
    is that limiting your experiences
    prevents you from being afraid.

Forgiveness ————————————————— 129
    is that you can forgive and remember.

Getting Wiser ————————————— 311
    is that you can forget what you know.

Good Will ——————————————— 299
    is that it begins with them.

Guilt ———————————————————— 65
    is that it compensates for something.

Habits ——————————————————— 247
    is that you recognize one
    when you see one.

A Matter of Choice

A fundamental misunderstanding about

Insight ———————————————— 93
   is that you recognize
   the messenger.

Jealousy ——————————————— 157
   is that they make you jealous.

Learning ——————————————— 4
   is that life has
   correct answers somewhere.

Love ————————————————— 135
   is that they have something
   to do with it.

Manifesting —————————————— 271
   is that it happens by accident.

Mastering ——————————————— 218
   is that it isn't possible.

Miracles ———————————————— 283
   is that they rarely happen.

Money ————————————————— 201
   is that it controls the quality
   of your life.

Mothers ———————————————— 175
   is that their only job is you.

A fundamental misunderstanding about

Parents ——————————————— 187
    is that your problem
    is their fault.

Perfect ——————————————— 87
    is that there is one
    right way to do and be.

Practicing —————————————— 106
    is that it gets over.

Problems ——————————————— 141
    is that what looks
    like one is one.

Risk ————————————————— 47
    is that risk is a
    negative proposition.

Selfishness ——————————————— 35
    is that loving yourself means
    you are selfish.

Sex ————————————————— 151
    is that it is about you.

Sexual Energy —————————————— 265
    is that it can only be expended
    by having sex.

A Matter of Choice

A fundamental misunderstanding about

Sharing ———————————————— 121
    is that they are supposed to.

Success ———————————————— 277
    is that you don't have any.

Taking Charge ————————————— 27
    is that you can't.

Thankful ———————————————— 305
    is that you can't be
    until it's better.

Thoughts ———————————————— 253
    is that no one
    knows your secrets.

Trust ————————————————— 83
    is that someone believes
    when you think they should.

Waking Up ———————————————— 21
    is that nothing happens
    while you are asleep.

Work ————————————————— 195
    is that it is something to do
    in the meantime.

A fundamental misunderstanding about

Worry ———————————————— 71
    is that you have to.

You ————————————————— 9
    is that you are what you know,
    what you have, or what you do.

Your Story ——————————————— 223
    is that it is the worst, the best,
    the most interesting, or
    the most tragic that
    has ever happened.

Your Word ——————————————— 99
    is that if you didn't mean it,
    it doesn't count.

From Phoenix Rising

Phoenix Rising is an idea, created by intention to teach people to live their lives on purpose. The Phoenix, a bird in Egyptian mythology, consumed itself by fire after five hundred years and rose renewed from its ashes. We believe that a new story in human affairs is beginning. We are committed to advancing the cause of human dignity and human growth by addressing old issues in new ways. We address the issues of self-esteem, meaningful work, and profound relationships. We teach people to live their lives deliberately.

It is our sincere wish that, no matter where you are in your process, you will find that *A Matter of Choice* speaks directly to you—encouraging you to learn, practice, and master life's lessons in order to manifest your greatness. Reaching the final chapter does not bring you to the end, but rather to your own deliberate new beginning.

Universal challenges have made it imperative that each individual begin to take responsibility for the quality of life on this planet. This idea necessitates an intervention in individual lives—a process that begins with you.

This book is a corollary to our previous work, *Living On Purpose*, which is available from Simon & Schuster in local bookstores everywhere.

Ordering Information

A Matter of Choice (paperback) $11.95

Partnering On Purpose (audio tape)   10.00
    approx. 1 hr. length

Beyond Burn Out (audio tape)   10.00
    approx. 45 min. length

                    Total $ _____

Illinois residents add 6.75% sales tax   _____

Postage and handling fee (add $2.00 for first item and .50 each additional item)   _____

Outside of continental United States (add ($1.50 to total postage fee)   _____

                Total Due $ _____

Send order and/or request to be on mailing list to

        Phoenix Rising Press
        P.O. Box 3088
        Glen Ellyn, Illinois 60138

                              Thank you.